LifeChange
S E R I E S

A NavPress Bible study on the book of

NEHEMIAH

NAVPRESS
A MINISTRY OF THE NAVIGATORS
P.O. Box 6000, Colorado Springs, CO 80934

The Navigators is an international Christian organiza-
tion. Jesus Christ gave His followers the Great Com-
mission to go and make disciples (Matthew 28:19).
The aim of The Navigators is to help fulfill that com-
mission by multiplying laborers for Christ in every
nation.

NavPress is the publishing ministry of The Navigators.
NavPress publications are tools to help Christians
grow. Although publications alone cannot make disciples or change lives, they can help believers learn
biblical discipleship, and apply what they learn to
their lives and ministries.

© 1985 by The Navigators
All rights reserved, including translation
ISBN: 0-89109-053-3
10538

Second printing, 1986

Most Scripture quotations are from the *Holy Bible:
New International Version* (NIV). Copyright © 1973,
1978, 1984, International Bible Society. Used by permission of Zondervan Bible Publishers. Other versions
used are the *New American Standard Bible* (NASB), ©
The Lockman Foundation 1960, 1962, 1963, 1968,
1971, 1972, 1973, 1975, 1977; and the *Revised Standard Version of the Bible* (RSV), copyrighted 1946, 1952
© 1971, 1973.

Printed in the United States of America

CONTENTS

ACKNOWLEDGMENTS

This LIFECHANGE study has been produced through the coordinated efforts of a team of Navigator Bible study developers and NavPress editorial staff, along with a nationwide network of fieldtesters.

SERIES EDITOR: KAREN HINCKLEY

HOW TO USE THIS STUDY

Objectives

Each guide in the LIFECHANGE series of Bible studies covers one book of the Bible. Although the LIFECHANGE guides vary with the individual books they explore, they share some common goals:

1. To provide you with a firm foundation of understanding and a thirst to return to the book;
2. To teach you by example how to study a book of the Bible without structured guides;
3. To give you all the historical background, word definitions, and explanatory notes you need, so that your only other reference is the Bible;
4. To help you grasp the message of the book as a whole;
5. To teach you how to let God's Word transform you into Christ's image.

Each lesson in this study is designed to take 60 to 90 minutes to complete on your own. The guide is based on the assumption that you are completing one lesson per week, but if time is limited you can do half a lesson per week or whatever amount allows you to be thorough.

Flexibility

LIFECHANGE guides are flexible, allowing you to adjust the quantity and depth of your study to meet your individual needs. The guide offers many optional questions in addition to the regular numbered questions. The optional questions, which appear in the margins of the study pages, include the following:

Optional Application. Nearly all application questions are optional; we hope you will do as many as you can without overcommitting yourself.

For Thought and Discussion. Beginning Bible students should be able to handle these, but even advanced students need to think about them. These questions frequently deal with ethical issues and other biblical principles. They often offer cross-references to spark thought, but the references do not give obvious answers. They are good for group discussions.

For Further Study. These include: a) cross-references that shed light on a topic the book discusses, and b) questions that delve deeper into the passage. You can omit them to shorten a lesson without missing a major point of the passage.

(Note: At the end of lessons three through thirteen you are given the option of outlining the passage just studied. Although the outline is optional, you will almost surely find it worthwhile.)

If you are meeting in a group, decide together which optional questions to prepare for each lesson, and how much of the lesson you will cover at the next meeting. Normally, the group leader should make this decision, but you might let each member choose his own application questions.

As you grow in your walk with God, you will find the LIFECHANGE guide growing with you—a helpful reference on a topic, a continuing challenge for application, a source of questions for many levels of growth.

Overview and Details

The guide begins with an overview of the book. The key to interpretation is context—what is the whole passage or book *about*?—and the key to context is purpose—what is the author's *aim* for the whole work? In lesson one you will lay the foundation for your study by asking yourself, Why did the author (and God) write the book? What did they want to accomplish? What is the book about?

Then, in lesson two, you will begin analyzing successive passages in detail. Thinking about how a paragraph fits into the overall goal of the book will help you to see its purpose. Its purpose will help you see its meaning. Frequently reviewing a chart or outline of the book will enable you to make these connections.

Finally, in the last lesson, you will review the whole book, returning to the big picture to see whether your view of it has changed after closer study. Review will also strengthen your grasp of major issues and give you an idea of how you have grown from your study.

Kinds of Questions

Bible study on your own—without a structured guide—follows a progression. First you observe: What does the passage *say*? Then you interpret: What does the passage *mean*? Lastly you apply: How does this truth affect my life? The act of wording a question for the guide nearly always makes it interpretation, however, so you may want to observe first yourself.

Some of the "how" and "why" questions will take some creative thinking, even prayer, to answer. Some are opinion questions without clearcut right answers; these will lend themselves to discussions and side studies.

Don't let your study become an exercise of knowledge alone. Treat the passage as God's Word, and stay in dialogue with Him as you study. Pray, "Lord, what do you want me to see here?" "Father, why is this true?" "Lord, how does

6

this apply to my life?"

It is important that you write down your answers. The act of writing clarifies your thinking and helps you to remember.

Meditating on verses is an option in several lessons. Its purpose is to let biblical truth sink into your inner convictions so that you will increasingly be able to act on this truth as a natural way of life. You may want to find a quiet place to spend five minutes each day repeating the verse(s) to yourself. Think about what each word, phrase, and sentence means to you. During the rest of the day, remind yourself of the verse(s) at intervals.

Study Aids

A list of reference materials, including a few notes of explanation to help you make good use of them, begins on page 125. This guide is designed to include enough background to let you interpret with just your Bible and the guide. Still, if you want more information on a subject or want to study a book on your own, try the references listed.

Scripture Versions

Unless otherwise indicated, the Bible quotations in this guide are from the New International Version of the Bible. Other versions cited are the Revised Standard Version (RSV) and the New American Standard Bible (NASB).

Use any translation you like for study, preferably more than one. A paraphrase, such as the Living Bible or the Good News Bible, is not accurate enough for study, but it can be helpful for comparison or devotional reading.

Memorizing and Meditating

A Psalmist wrote, "I have hidden your word in my heart that I might not sin against you" (Psalm 119:11). If you write down a verse or passage that challenges or encourages you, and reflect on it often for a week or more, you will find it beginning to affect your motives and actions. We forget quickly what we read once; we remember what we ponder.

When you find a significant verse or passage, you might copy it onto a card to keep with you. Set aside five minutes during each day just to think about what the passage might mean in your life. Recite it over to yourself, exploring its meaning. Then, return to your passage as often as you can during your day, for a brief review. You will soon find it coming to mind spontaneously.

For Group Study

A group of four to ten people allows the richest discussions, but you can adapt this guide for other sized groups. It will suit a wide range of group types, such as home Bible studies, growth groups, youth groups, and businessmen's studies. Both new and experienced Bible students, new and mature Christians, will benefit from the guide. You can omit or leave for later years any questions you find too easy or too hard.

The guide is intended to lead a group through one lesson per week. However, feel free to split lessons if you want to discuss them more thoroughly. Or, omit some questions in a lesson if preparation or discussion time is limited. You can always return to this guide for personal study later on. You will be able to discuss only a few questions at length, so choose some for discussion and others for background. Make time at each discussion for members to ask about anything that gave them trouble.

Each lesson in the guide ends with a section called *For the Group*. These sections give advice on how to focus a discussion, how you might apply the lesson in your group, how you might shorten a lesson, and so on. The group leader should read each *For the Group* at least a week ahead so that he or she can tell the group how to prepare for the next lesson.

Each member should prepare for a meeting by writing answers for all the background and discussion questions to be covered. If the group decides not to take an hour per week for private preparation, then expect to take at least two meetings per lesson to work through the questions. Application will be very difficult, however, without private thought and prayer.

Two reasons for studying in a group are accountability and support. When each member commits in front of the rest to seek growth in an area of life, you can pray with one another, listen jointly for God's guidance, help one another to resist temptation, assure each other that the other's growth matters to you, use the group to practice spiritual principles, and so on. Pray about one another's commitments and needs at most meetings. Spend the first few minutes of each meeting sharing any results from applications prompted by previous lessons. Then discuss new applications toward the end of the meeting. Follow such sharing with prayer for these and other needs.

If you write down each other's applications and prayer requests, you are more likely to remember to pray for them during the week, ask about them next meeting, and notice answered prayers. You might want to get a notebook for prayer requests and discussion notes.

Notes taken during discussion will help you to remember, follow up on ideas, stay on the subject, and clarify a total view of an issue. But don't let note-taking keep you from participating. Some groups choose one member at each meeting to take notes. Then someone copies the notes and distributes them at the next meeting. Rotating these tasks can help include people. Some groups have someone take notes on a large pad of paper or erasable marker board (preformed shower wallboard works well), so that everyone can see what has been recorded.

Page 127 lists some good sources of counsel for leading group studies. The *Small Group Letter,* published by NavPress, is unique, offering insights from experienced leaders each month.

HISTORICAL BACKGROUND

Map of Persian Empire in Nehemiah's Time

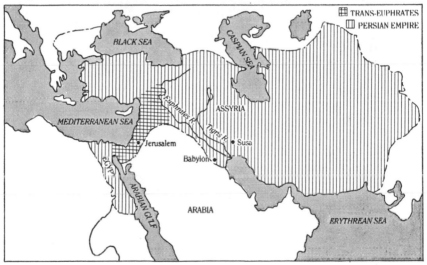

Comfort, comfort my people, says your God.
Speak tenderly to Jerusalem, and proclaim to her
    that her hard service has been completed,
    that her sin has been paid for,
    that she has received from the LORD'S hand
        double for all her sins.
A voice of one calling:
    "In the desert prepare the way for the LORD;
    make straight in the wilderness a highway for our God."
                    Isaiah 40:1-3

So Isaiah prophesied the end of Judah's exile from the promised land.

9

NEHEMIAH TIMELINE

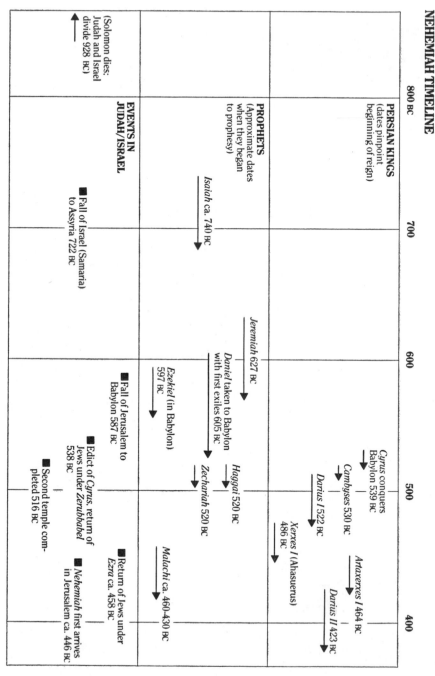

	800 BC	700	600	500	400
PERSIAN KINGS (dates pinpoint beginning of reign)				Cyrus conquers Babylon 539 BC; Cambyses 530 BC; Darius I 522 BC; Xerxes I (Ahasuerus) 486 BC; Artaxerxes I 464 BC; Darius II 423 BC	
PROPHETS (Approximate dates when they began to prophesy)		Isaiah ca. 740 BC	Jeremiah 627 BC; Daniel taken to Babylon with first exiles 605 BC; Ezekiel (in Babylon) 597 BC	Haggai 520 BC; Zechariah 520 BC	Malachi ca. 460-430 BC
EVENTS IN JUDAH/ISRAEL	(Solomon dies; Judah and Israel divide 928 BC)	■ Fall of Israel (Samaria) to Assyria 722 BC	■ Fall of Jerusalem to Babylon 587 BC	■ Edict of Cyrus, return of Jews under Zerubbabel 538 BC; ■ Second temple completed 516 BC	■ Return of Jews under Ezra ca. 458 BC; ■ Nehemiah first arrives in Jerusalem ca. 446 BC

10

The fall of Israel

Solomon's kingdom split in two after his death in 928 BC. For two hundred years the northern kingdom of Israel (Samaria) drifted further and further from the Lord.[1] At last He abandoned the nation to conquest by Assyria in 722 BC.

To frustrate national allegiances, Assyria scattered conquered families all over the Near East. Samaria was emptied of Israelites and refilled with people who worshiped many gods. The newcomers adopted the Lord, the local god, alongside their ancestral customs and gods.

The fall of Judah

The southern kingdom of Judah was scarcely more faithful to the Lord than Israel. Judah survived the Assyrian threat through repentance, but it fell prey a century later to Assyria's successor, Babylon. Part of Judah's noble class was exiled to Babylon in 605 BC. Jerusalem was captured and its king deported in 597. Then, after its government tried to rebel, Jerusalem was finally sacked and burned in 587. The conquerors marched all but the poorest of the city's inhabitants back to Babylon, along with the valuables of the ruined Temple. Like the Samaritans, the few Israelites left in Judah adopted the customs of their pagan neighbors alongside worship of the Lord.

Cyrus sends Zerubbabel

Babylon went the way of Assyria however, falling to the Persian king Cyrus in 539. Cyrus viewed politics and religion very differently from his predecessors. He wanted to rule diverse peoples as a political unit while respecting their varied customs and beliefs. Convinced that sheer force could not make a large empire stable, he sought acceptance through toleration. Instead of forcing everyone to worship Persian gods, Cyrus encouraged each people to seek its own gods' favor for him. He sent people back to their homelands, returned confiscated religious objects, and financed the rebuilding of temples. This policy was so successful that Cyrus's successors continued it.

One of the many peoples who benefited from this policy was the group from Judah. These exiles called themselves Jews—members of the tribes of Judah, Benjamin, and Levi; inheritors of the Lord's promises to Israel, the "remnant" foretold by Isaiah (Isaiah 10:20-22). The Jews considered themselves distinct not only from ethnic Canaanites and Persians, but also from those residents of Samaria and Judah who worshiped the Lord according to local customs and who had not gone through the purging of the exile. Allegiance to the Lord alone, proven in a life led according to His instruction, was the sign of a true Jew.

Cyrus commanded the first return of Jews to Jerusalem in 538 BC. He provided money for the expedition and for rebuilding the Temple, and he restored the Temple valuables. The Jews under Zerubbabel returned 67 years after the first exiles were taken from Judah in 605; Jeremiah's prophecy of 70 years of exile (Jeremiah 29:10) was fulfilled.

11

After some conflict with the people who had been living around Jerusalem, Zerubbabel's group finally completed the Temple in 516. (Chapters 1-6 of the book of Ezra, and the books of Haggai and Zechariah recount these events.)

Artaxerxes sends Ezra

Confusion about how the Lord would be worshiped and how Jews would live evidently caused strife in Judah, for the Persian king Artaxerxes I sent another party of Jews under Ezra "to enforce the law of Moses."[2] When Ezra and his group arrived in Jerusalem in 458, they found a cold welcome from non-Jews and from Jews who were assimilating into the dominant culture. The men who held political, social, religious, or economic power naturally resented the threat to their positions.

Ezra was able to enforce the law to some extent, but the local leaders complained to Artaxerxes that Ezra's party was rebelling against Persia. In response, Artaxerxes authorized the adversaries "to make these men stop work, that the city may not be rebuilt until a decree is issued by me" (Ezra 4:21 NASB). Nehemiah 1:3 suggests that Ezra's opponents not only stopped the building but also destroyed what had been begun. Without imperial protection, the reformers were at the mercy of the powerful assimilated men.

Artaxerxes sends Nehemiah

This news reached Nehemiah in November-December 446 BC (1:1). The Persian regime was so open to people of non-Persian blood and religion that this devout Jew was cupbearer (1:11) to Artaxerxes himself. A cupbearer, whose primary duty was to choose and taste the king's wine to assure that it was not poisoned, was a trusted official. He was a man of great influence because he had so much access to the ruler. This man's response to the news of the Jerusalem mission's tragedy is the subject of the book of Nehemiah.

Most of the book is taken from Nehemiah's own memoirs. It is an account of people doing God's work despite threats to their survival and of return to faithfulness after laxity—an account mostly from the man who led the work.

1. The God of Israel gave Himself the name YHWH in Exodus 3:14. In most English translations of the Bible, the name of God is written as "the LORD," following the Jewish belief that the name of God is too holy to be spoken. Others write "Jehovah" or "Yahweh." We will call Him "the Lord" in this study.
2. Derek Kidner, *Ezra and Nehemiah, an Introduction and Commentary,* (Downers Grove, Illinois: InterVarsity Press, 1979), page 13. By *law of Moses* we mean the first five books of the Christian Old Testament, sometimes called the *Pentateuch*. The Jews believed God had taught these books to Moses in the wilderness of Sinai. The Hebrew word for these books, *Torah*, means "teaching" or "instruction" as well as "law," for the Torah contained not only commands about behavior but also teaching about God's character and His dealings with people in history. Past history told the Jews their identity and God's promises for their present and future. Along with the written Torah went an oral tradition of interpreting it, a tradition in which Ezra, as a scribe, was skilled.

OVERVIEW

The best start toward understanding a book of Scripture is to read it through first for an overall sense of what the author is trying to say. Besides, Nehemiah is a good story, and so is best appreciated when read straight through for its humor, suspense, and development of plot and character. So before you get lost in details, read the book through as you would read a short story. (You might want to read it several times, perhaps in different translations.)

1. A good story lets you get to know characters. Tell a little about each of the main characters in Nehemiah.

   Nehemiah _____

   _____

   _____

   _____

   Artaxerxes _____

   _____

   _____

   Sanballat _____

   _____

   _____

Tobiah _____

_____

_____

_____

Eliashib _____

_____

_____

_____

2. Repetition is a clue to the ideas and objects an author thinks are most important to his message. List any key words or phrases which recur in the story.

_____

_____

_____

_____

3. You get to know the point of a story by studying the actions of the characters.

a. Toward what goals do the characters (and God) appear to work in this story?

Nehemiah _____

_____

_____

_____

Sanballat and Tobiah _____

_____

_____

_____

the Jews _____

_____

_____

_____

God _____

_____

_____

_____

b. What conflicts produce the action (people vs. people, people vs. things, etc.)?

_____

_____

_____

_____

_____

4. An outline of the main sections of a book will help you see how the story develops. What do you think are the major sections of Nehemiah? Below, give verse references and titles for them. Think big: try to reduce the book to between two and six main sections.

1:1- _____

_____

_____

_____

_____

_____

_____

_____

_____

5. What main ideas or themes do you think this book
   is intended to teach? (Examples: obedience; how
   God fulfills His plan in history.)

_____

_____

_____

_____

_____

_____

_____

6. A key to understanding a book of the Bible is iden-
   tifying its *purpose* (although a given book may
   have several purposes). Try to state at least one
   major purpose of the book of Nehemiah. (Why do
   you think Nehemiah wrote the book? What do you
   think God wants us to learn from it?)

_____

_____

_____

_____

_____

7. Nehemiah assumes that the reader knows a great
   deal about the times he lived in—about Persian
   politics, Near Eastern geography, Jewish customs,

etc. The Historical Background (pages 9-12)
addresses some of those matters. (Others are discussed later in the study guide. The bibliography
on pages 125-128 lists some places where you may
find more complete answers.) If you have not
already done so, read the Historical Background in
order to familiarize yourself with the context in
which the events of the book of Nehemiah took
place.

8. From the Historical Background and from Nehemiah's book, have you discovered anything about
Nehemiah's world, in Persia or Judah, that is
remarkably like or unlike your own? Explain.

_____

_____

_____

_____

_____

_____

_____

_____

_____

_____

_____

Study Skill—Application
The last step of Bible study is asking yourself,
"What difference should this passage make in
my life? How should it make me think or act?"
Application will require time, thought, prayer,
and perhaps even discussion with another person. You may find it more productive to concen-
trate on one specific application, giving it careful thought and prayer, than to list several
potential applications without really reflecting
on them or committing yourself to them. One
step actually taken is more important than
many steps supported only by good intentions!

9. Does your first reading suggest any ways that Nehemiah's book applies to you? If so, explain briefly in what ways it applies and how you might respond to it.

_____

_____

_____

_____

_____

_____

_____

_____

10. In your initial reading of the book of Nehemiah, you may have come across concepts you'd like clarified, or you may have questions you'd like answered as you go deeper into this study. While your thoughts are still fresh, you may want to jot down your questions here to serve as personal objectives for your investigation of this book.

_____

_____

_____

_____

_____

_____

_____

_____

As you study Nehemiah more closely, it will be important to keep the big picture in mind. Refer often to questions 4 and 6 of this lesson.

For the group

Not everyone is good at outlining and overviews.
Those in your group who found these tasks easy might
describe how they approached the tasks. There are no
"right" divisions of the book—why do you prefer one
way to another? (The chart on page 20 gives one view
of the major sections. How do your divisions compare
with that view?)

If you do not know each other well, you might
spend some time in your next few meetings establish-
ing trust, common ground, and a sense of where each
person is coming from and what he or she hopes to
gain from the study. This may help you later with honest discussion on how Nehemiah applies to each of
you. This meeting, share something of your
histories—perhaps what you remember about being
nine years old, or the first place you lived. Then discuss question 9.

Chart of Nehemiah

Purpose: To show how God used Nehemiah to restore His holy city to holy use.

Nehemiah prepares for his mission. 1:1 2:8	1:1-11 Nehemiah prays for God's people.
	2:1-8 Nehemiah speaks to the king.
Nehemiah regathers God's people and leads them in rebuilding God's city. 2:9 6:19	2:9-20 Nehemiah convinces the Jews to rebuild the wall.
	3:1-32 The Jews build.
	4:1-23 The builders resist opposition.
	5:1-19 Nehemiah rights injustices among the Jews.
	6:1-19 Nehemiah resists opposition.
Nehemiah prepares to repopulate God's city. 7:1 7:72	7:1-72 Nehemiah prepares to repopulate the city. (census)
God's people rededicate themselves to God. 7:73 10:39	7:73-8:12 Ezra reads the Law.
	8:13-18 The Jews keep the Feast of Tabernacles.
	9:1-38 The Jews confess sin.
	10:1-39 The Jews commit to the Lord.
God's people live and celebrate in God's city. 11:1 13:3	11:1-12:26 (Nehemiah inserts a list of leaders in Jerusalem and Judah.)
	12:27-13:3 The Jews dedicate the wall.
Nehemiah cleanses abuses. 13:4 13:31	13:4-31 Nehemiah returns after 12 years and restores holy obedience.

NEHEMIAH 1:1-11

A Plea for Help

Read through the whole passage at least once before approaching the questions. You may also want to skim the lesson—noticing subtitles, definitions, etc.— before beginning to answer any of the questions. Keep in mind the overview of the book you got in lesson 1.

For Further Study: To learn more about the exile, read 2 Kings 24:1-25:30, Ezra, Psalms 42, 79, 84, Lamentations, Ezekiel, or Daniel.

Bad news (1:1-4)

1. What was the "exile" (NASB: "captivity") discussed in the first few verses of Nehemiah? See page 11.

_____

_____

_____

> **Study Skill—Cross-References**
> Other passages of Scripture can often shed light on what you are studying. These are called **cross-references.**

2. What can we learn about Nehemiah (his character, values, etc.) from his reaction to the news of disaster (verse 4)?

_____

_____

_____

_____

_____

_____

_____

_____

Prayer (1:5-11)

Covenant: (verse 5). The relationship between God and His people, the Jews. The whole history of Israel was the history of the covenant. It was not an agreement between equals but the gracious gift of a sovereign to his subjects. Its main content was God's promises to multiply Israel, to give the people the land of Canaan, to protect them, and to make them an example to the nations of God's goodness. In return the Jews were to fear, love, serve, and obey God alone.

Love: (verse 5). "Lovingkindness" in NASB. The attitude expected of covenanting parties toward one another. On God's side, it meant unfailing loyalty: constant provision of needs, protection from danger, and restoration of the nation once the people had repented from disobedience. It included forgiveness and mercy, for its essence was God's bending to love His creatures, even the unrepentant. The people's response was to be "covenant love" toward God and each other.

3. Study Nehemiah's prayer in 1:5-11.

   a. Give a short label to each part of this prayer, according to the sections you see it falling into. Write the verse reference first; then put your title, or label, next to it.

_____

_____

_____

_____

_____

_____

_____

_____

_____

b. Can you discover any elements in Nehemiah's prayer that you might find useful as a model for your own prayer life? If so, what are they, and how might you incorporate them?

_____

_____

_____

_____

_____

_____

4. List everything you observe from verses 5-11 about the character of God.

_____

_____

_____

_____

_____

_____

Optional Application: Are there any needs of your nation, the Church, or the world that move you as Nehemiah was moved by his people's need? What might they be?

_____

_____

_____

_____

_____

_____

Study Skill—Summarizing the Passage

You will remember more of a narrative book like Nehemiah if you summarize the main events of each passage as you study it. The chart on page 20 gives an example.

Following Nehemiah's example

Reread the box on application on page 17. The two "Optional Application" questions on this and the following page suggest some ways to apply 1:1-11. If neither of these suits you, questions 10 and 11 invite you to come up with your own applications.

Study Skill—Themes and Principles

In your overview, you looked for themes in Nehemiah's book so that you could watch for them in further study. Questions 3 and 5-9 of this lesson pursue one theme of the book— prayer. From these questions you could draw principles that apply to prayer in any age.

Now, question 10 asks you to list principles on other themes as well as prayer. Think about other lessons from Nehemiah's life that can be found in chapter 1. What kinds of insights can **you** discover that apply to all believers—not just to Nehemiah and his times? (Some themes you might think about are: obedience; qualities of a leader; facing opposition; God acting in history to fulfill His plan; God's sovereignty; God's faithfulness; God's holy people—pure and separate; Scripture— revelation and command; how spiritual revival happens.)

---

10. What other principles, on prayer or other topics, do you find in 1:1-11 that apply to Christians today?

_____

_____

_____

_____

_____

_____

_____

_____

11. Have you discovered a principle or insight that you think God may want you to apply to your own life? If so, jot it down here, along with one initial step that could help you get going in this area.

_____

_____

_____

_____

_____

_____

_____

_____

12. List any questions you have about 1:1-11.

_____

_____

_____

_____

Optional Application: Nehemiah prayed because he had a great burden for a specific need to carry out God's will. Can you discern a specific need for accomplishing God's purposes that God might be giving you a burden to pray for? What else can you do to discover what God wants you to pray into being? What can you do to learn how He wants to use you to accomplish His ends? Try to think of a specific course of action.

For the group

Focus on what you learn from 1:1-11 about a) Nehemiah; b) God; and c) prayer.

Provide time for members to ask questions about
anything they did not understand. Try to make plans
for answering those questions either from the resources listed on pages 125-128, from further Bible study,
or from someone outside the group. You might choose
a group member to pursue each question. Or, you
could decide to keep your questions in front of you as
you continue with this study, to see if you can answer
them as you progress with the book of Nehemiah.

Nehemiah faithfully lifted up in prayer his burden
for the restoration of Jerusalem. Pray together about
what burdens God might have you bear to Him in
prayer. If some needs are already clear to you, begin
praying about them as Nehemiah did.

Consider taking time again to share something of
your histories. Understanding each other will make
sharing about applications easier.

> 'Praying for particular things,' said I, 'always seems to
> me like advising God how to run the world. Wouldn't it
> be wiser to assume that He knows best?' 'On the same
> principle,' said he, 'I suppose you never ask a man next
> to you to pass the salt, because God knows best
> whether you ought to have salt or not. And I suppose
> you never take an umbrella, because God knows best
> whether you ought to be wet or dry.' 'That's quite dif-
> ferent,' I protested. 'I don't see why,' said he. 'The odd
> thing is that He should let us influence the course of
> events at all. But since He lets us do it in one way I
> don't see why He shouldn't let us do it in the other.'[1]

1. C.S. Lewis, *God in the Dock, Essays on Theology and Ethics*,
   (Grand Rapids, Michigan: William B. Eerdmans Publishing
   Company, 1970), page 217.

NEHEMIAH 2:1-8

A Risk

Read through 2:1-8 before beginning the questions. Think about how 2:1-8 develops the themes of the book.

Nisan: (verse 1). April; that is, four months later.

1. What was the "success" for which Nehemiah prayed in 1:11? (Look for the answer in these first eight verses of chapter 2.)

_____

_____

_____

_____

2. a. Nehemiah was approaching the very king who had ordered the apparent rebels to cease building (see page 12), and an oriental emperor commonly executed officials who displeased him. What can you tell about Nehemiah's character from his encounter with King Artaxerxes?

_____

_____

_____

For Further Study:
Proverbs 21:1 asserts God's sovereignty over secular authorities. To further explore how God works through secular governments, see Romans 13:1-7 and 1 Peter 2:12-20. Or, compare Nehemiah's strategy for dealing with his king to John 14:12-13. How might these principles apply today?

For Thought and Discussion: Think about the risks that Nehemiah took to pursue his goal.
a. What risks do committed Christians encounter today in their work for God's Kingdom?
b. What risks might God be leading you to take in pursuing His goals? What are your resources for enduring these risks?

b. Why do you think Nehemiah took this risk?

_____

_____

_____

_____

_____

_____

_____

Trans-Euphrates: (verse 7). See the map on page 9. Trans-Euphrates ("beyond the River") comprised all of Syria and Palestine. A provincial governor administered it, and district governors of Samaria, Judah, Ammon, etc. worked under him.[1]

---

3. Most commentators think "for some days" in 1:4 means that Nehemiah prayed from Kislev, when he received the bad news, to Nisan, when he prayed as in 1:11 and acted as in 2:1-8.[2] Why do you suppose Nehemiah might have spent four months praying about the situation in Jerusalem? Why did he not act at once?

_____

_____

_____

_____

_____

_____

4. a. Compare the prayer in 1:5-11 with that of 2:4, using the chart on the next page.

30

1:5-11	2:4
Length and nature of the prayer	
Where it took place	
Purpose	

Optional Application: a. What are your greatest difficulties in praying? Think about external as well as internal factors—for example, circumstances that hinder you, attitudes that you need to work through, or priorities that may be out of place.

b. What might you do to overcome those difficulties and pray more powerfully?

b. How did these two kinds of prayer complement each other?

_____

_____

_____

_____

_____

_____

For Thought and Discussion: What can you conclude from 2:1-8 about how God works in the lives of His people, the Church, or your nation?

5. What connections between prayer and action does this passage (2:1-8) show?

_____

_____

_____

_____

_____

_____

6. Try to summarize how you think 2:1-8 shows some of the themes and purposes you identified in lesson one, questions 5 and 6.

_____

_____

_____

_____

_____

_____

_____

Study Skill—Charting Themes

You will grasp the book better if you can see how each passage relates to the book's themes and purposes. For instance, one theme of Nehemiah's book is godly obedience. So, you could say that 2:1-8 shows Nehemiah responding obediently by seeking a new job—despite risks and because of prayer.

The chart on page 20 breaks the book into major sections and then summarizes the main events of each passage. You could use the same format to trace a theme through the book. The chart on pages 34-35 is blank. As you move through the book of Nehemiah, consider using this chart to trace one or more themes. You could make several charts, one for each theme that interests you.

Following Nehemiah's example

7. List any principles (about obedience, leadership, etc.) you learned from 2:1-8 that you think are relevant today.

_____

_____

_____

_____

_____

_____

_____

_____

Optional Application: Take time today, and each day for the next week, to pray about something you discovered or decided while working through this lesson. After a few days, write down here a summary of your prayer.

8. Has God revealed to you recently any pressing concerns to carry before Him in prayer? If so, write down what they are, as well as a practical plan for how you could accomplish this task of prayer.

_____

_____

_____

_____

_____

_____

_____

_____

9. List any questions you have about this lesson.

_____

_____

Chart of Nehemiah

Theme:

	1:1-11
	2:1-8
	2:9-20
	3:1-32
	4:1-23
	5:1-19
	6:1-19

	7:1-72
	7:73-8:12
	8:13-18
	9:1-38
	10:1-39
	11:1-12:26
	12:27-13:3
	13:4-31

For Further Study:
Rich insights into Scripture grow from keen observation, a learned skill.

a. Reread 2:1-8, and on another sheet of paper list as many observations as you can about the passage. Try for at least thirty. Sometimes seemingly trivial observations lead to important truths.

b. These observations should suggest questions like those in the guide. List ten questions (who, what, when, where, how, why) that your observations suggest. If you can't answer them now, come back to them after you have worked through more of Nehemiah.

For the group

Key concepts in this passage are: a) the connection between prayer and action; and b) Nehemiah's character traits.

Discuss any leadings you feel for prayer or for risky action. You may have varying convictions about individual tasks, or several of you may share one. Pray together about these leadings. Finally, *encourage* one another to pray and to act on what you hear in prayer.

Make sure that everyone understands how to relate a passage to the themes of the whole book. Everyone should find a statement of purpose and a list of themes that satisfies him, but you need not all agree.

"Let us consider how we may spur one another on toward love and good deeds."
Hebrews 10:24

Rebellion under Artaxerxes

Cyrus was a strong and popular king, but his successors struggled to keep control of his empire. Under Artaxerxes there was trouble everywhere. The Arabs south of Judah refused to pay tribute. Egypt revolted in 459 BC; a year later Ezra was sent to Judah to enforce Jewish and Persian law. The governor of Trans-Euphrates put down the Egyptian revolt in 454, but he himself rebelled against Persia in 448. Subjects in Judah, Samaria, and Ammon were bickering for power.

In the midst of this uproar, the people of Jerusalem understandably wanted a wall for protection, but Artaxerxes equally understandably believed the charge that the Jews were another group of rebels. He was probably glad to send a trusted servant like Nehemiah to assure Judah's order and loyalty while he quelled the Egyptian and Arab rebellions.

---

1. Kidner, page 52.
2. Kidner, page 80.

NEHEMIAH 2:9-20

To Jerusalem

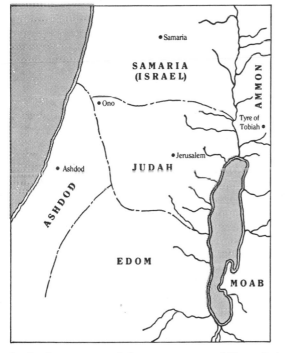

Again, be sure to read the passage several times first. Then glance through the lesson's subtitles and questions. As in lesson 2, the subtitles show one way to label the paragraphs of the passage. Giving a title to each paragraph helps you to grasp its content; try making up paragraph titles when you study a book on your own.

As you study, keep asking yourself how the passage reflects Nehemiah's themes and purposes.

Arrival (2:9-16)

Nehemiah did not say anything about the dangers and discomfort of his travel from Susa to Jerusalem. However, you may imagine them from the distance he covered on a horse or camel and from his need of an army escort (verse 9).

1. a. Artaxerxes had given Nehemiah authority to carry out his plans by making him governor of Judah (5:14). Why do you think Nehemiah abandoned an influential and comfortable job with the king to take charge of a backwater province boiling with dissension (verses 11-12)?

   _____

   _____

   _____

   _____

   b. What does that decision tell you about his priorities?

   _____

   _____

   _____

   _____

Sanballat (verse 10) is known from another document to have been governor of Samaria. Until Nehemiah was appointed, Judah had been part of Sanballat's province. *Tobiah* was a common name in a powerful family in Ammon (see map, page 37). The name was Jewish, so Tobiah was a Jew by blood appointed as an official in Ammon.

38

2. Why do you think these two men, one of them even a Jew, were so "disturbed" (verse 10) when a new governor of Judah arrived in this style?

_____

_____

_____

_____

_____

By *Jews* (verse 16), Nehemiah meant all those who were neither priests, nobles, nor officials. He did not mention the differences among the Jews. Some had accompanied Ezra from Babylon in 458 BC to restore the worship of the Lord according to Torah. These people would have welcomed the king's change of heart, for they had just tried and failed to rebuild the wall. Still, they already had their own leaders and methods, and had never seen Nehemiah before.

Other Jews were grandchildren of those who had followed Zerubbabel from Babylon in 538 BC. These had assimilated into the mixed Judean culture; many had pagan wives and even mothers, few kept Torah, and most worshiped the Lord alongside other gods.

Finally, there were a few Jews (such as Tobiah?) whose ancestors had never gone into exile. These were perhaps the most assimilated.

3. From the information above and on page 12, can you guess why Nehemiah chose to

arrive in Judah with an escort and letters from the king (verse 9)?

_____

_____

_____

_____

spend three days in Jerusalem without telling
anyone his plans (verse 16)?

_____

_____

_____

survey the walls at night with a few selected
friends (verse 12)?

_____

_____

_____

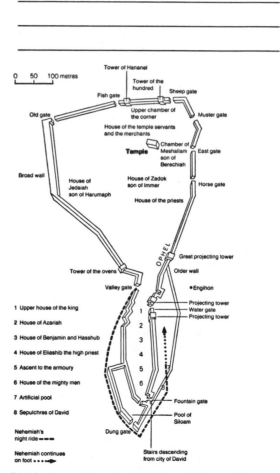

Taken from *Ezra and Nehemiah* by Derek Kidner. © 1979 by Derek Kidner
and used by permission of InterVarsity Press, Downers Grove, IL 60515.

4. Summarize what Nehemiah found when he inspected the walls (verses 13-15).

_____

_____

_____

_____

Persuasion and responses (2:17-20)

5. Nehemiah gave the Jews three reasons why they should try again to rebuild the wall. First, he said that the ruins were a "disgrace" (NASB: "reproach," verse 17). Why would he have characterized the situation in this way? (See Lamentations 2:15-18.)

_____

_____

_____

_____

_____

6. Explain the other encouragements for rebuilding that Nehemiah gave the Jews (Nehemiah 2:18).

a. _____

_____

_____

b. _____

_____

_____

7. Consider Nehemiah's recruitment effort (see verses 16-18). From the people's consent to follow this man they had known for only three days, in a

Optional Application: Do any of the three reasons you named in question 5 encourage you to get involved in some "good work" to build God's Kingdom? What would *your* reasons be, and how might you discover what your contribution could be?

project that had failed once already, what do you learn about

Nehemiah? _____

_____

_____

_____

_____

_____

the people? _____

_____

_____

_____

_____

_____

God's involvement in the affair? _____

_____

_____

_____

_____

8. *Geshem* (verse 19) apparently headed "a league of Arabian tribes which took control of Moab and Edom . . . together with part of Arabia and the approaches to Egypt . . . ."[1] Look at the map on page 37. Assuming that the territories controlled by Sanballat, Tobiah, and Geshem were all hostile to Nehemiah, describe the situation of Judah and its new governor.

_____

_____

_____

_____

42

The first challenge (2:19-20)

For Further Study:
Summarize one of your
answers in question
12 in your chart on
pages 34-35.

9. a. How did Nehemiah's enemies initially try to
   discourage him and his followers (verse 19)?

   _____

   _____

   _____

   _____

   b. Why do you think they did not use force at
   once? (See verse 9.)

   _____

   _____

   _____

   _____

10. In verse 20, Nehemiah rejected his enemies
    harshly. Why do you think he did so? (What do
    you learn about him from verse 20?)

    _____

    _____

    _____

    _____

11. In whom did Nehemiah trust for success (verse
    20)?

    _____

    _____

12. How does 2:9-20 reflect the themes of the book?
    Choose two or more of the themes listed below, or
    write about some other theme in the passage.

    leadership _____

    _____

43

**Optional
Application:** Consider
the attitudes displayed
by Nehemiah and the
Jews in 2:9-20.
a. Is there one
that you would like to
develop or strengthen
in your life? If so, jot it
down here.

b. Write out the
verse that discusses
that attitude. Memo-
rize and then meditate
on the verse daily for
the next week, pray for
the attitude, and look
for ways to practice it.

_____

_____

_____

_____

_____

16. List any questions you have about this passage.

_____

_____

_____

_____

_____

Study Skill—Application
Applying biblical truth to your life is often easier
if you share progress and problems with
another Christian periodically. For instance, if
you are trying to overcome difficulties in praying, you might want to meet with someone
weekly to pray with you, explore what inside and
outside you is hindering you from prayer,
search the Bible for guidance, etc. Whether you
want to take on a project or acquire a character
trait, that other person can be one of the Holy
Spirit's channels for grace. Another Christian
can help you stay committed while you are rely-
ing on God's power to work through you.

For the group

This passage shows a wise and godly leader in action.
To learn some principles for your own ministries,
observe what Nehemiah did and then interpret why he
did it. Also discuss how the passage reflects the book's
themes and purposes.

Questions 13-15, and the optional questions

in this lesson, are for discussion. You probably will not find simple solutions for any of them. You may not cover more than one or two in one meeting, so choose those that seem most relevant to you.

Try to save time for members to share how they are applying 2:9-20 to themselves.

Optional Application: Has there been a discovery from your study of 2:9-20 that prompts any additional response from you? If so, write down your own suggested application for it.

The Struggles of the Returned Exiles

Unlike Assyria in Samaria, Babylon had not imported subjects from across her empire when she took the Jews from Judah in 587 BC. Thus, there was room for the returnees in 538. However, Edomites had moved north from Edom under pressure from immigration from the south and west. Also, the poorest Jews had not been exiled, and they had taken title to all available land. They and some Persian appointees held all the local offices. So, the returning exiles had to cultivate land with no clear title to it on sufferance from their neighbors. But the exiles, zealous for pure worship of the Lord, alienated the never-exiled by declaring them unworthy for the pure to worship or even eat with. They wanted to be a strong community of God's servants, but they lacked good leadership. Then on top of legal squabbles, the fickle Judean weather—where flood rains followed months of drought—made crop failures frequent. Thus, the restoration of Zion slowed to a halt as the returnees grew preoccupied with survival. (See also the books of Ezra, Haggai, and Zechariah.)[2]

1. Kidner, page 84.
2. Kidner, page 8.

NEHEMIAH 3:1-4:23

Construction Begins

Read these two chapters through before beginning
your study. Do you think the subtitles of the lesson
capture the essence of the passages? How could you
improve them?

Cooperation (3:1-32)

In chapter 3 Nehemiah recorded the names and/or
occupations of those who led the building of each section of the wall. (If your time is limited, chapter 3 is a
better chapter to skim or skip than others.)

Levites: (verse 17). God had appointed the tribe of Levi
to care for the temple and its furnishings. Only
Levites could serve the priests, who performed the
actual sacrifices (Numbers 3:5-13). God had
appointed one branch of that tribe, the family of
Aaron, to be the priests.

---

1. Notice the classes of people who worked side by
   side at hard manual labor on the wall. What sorts
   of people are mentioned in each of the following
   sets of verses?

   3:8,31-32 _____

   _____

3:26 _____

_____

3:17 _____

_____

3:9,12,14-19 _____

_____

2. a. Why do you think the nobles of Tekoa refused to help (verse 5)?

_____

_____

_____

_____

  b. What would have happened if more people had felt that way?

_____

_____

_____

_____

3. a. What attitudes that the builders displayed in chapter 3 should Christians adopt when working together?

_____

_____

_____

50

_____

_____

b. What attitudes should Christians avoid?

_____

_____

_____

_____

_____

Optional Application: Can you think of some ways you could apply any of the builders' attitudes this week? If so, describe at least one first step you could take to carry this out.

The second challenge: ridicule (4:1-6)

The enemies' first attempt to discourage the builders failed (see 2:19-20). Nehemiah recorded another attempt in this passage.

_____

"Will they offer sacrifices?" (verse 2) probably means "Are these fanatics going to *pray* the wall up? It's their only hope!"[1]

_____

4. Summarize the faults Sanballat and Tobiah found with the building project.

   Sanballat (4:2) _____

   _____

   _____

   _____

   _____

   Tobiah (4:3) _____

   _____

   _____

   _____

5. To whom did they voice their criticisms (verse 2)?

_____

_____

_____

6. Why do you think they spoke to that audience instead of to Nehemiah privately? (What seems to have been their goal?)

_____

_____

_____

_____

_____

7. Do you think any of Sanballat's and Tobiah's comments were reasonable? Why or why not?

_____

_____

8. What do you learn about the builders from their response to ridicule (Nehemiah 4:6)?

_____

_____

_____

_____

_____

_____

The third challenge: a plot of force
(4:7-23)

Understand the threat of verses 7-8, and 11. (Recall from lesson 4, question 8 the danger that so many hostile people posed to the Jews.)

9. Name Nehemiah's two immediate responses to the threat of armed attack (verse 9).

a. _____

_____

b. _____

_____

10. What do these responses, in this order, reveal about him?

_____

_____

_____

_____

_____

_____

11. Name the builders' two fears in verses 10 and 12.

verse 10 _____

_____

_____

verse 12 _____

_____

_____

12. How did Nehemiah encourage them?

action (verse 13) _____

_____

_____

reminder (verse 14) _____

_____

_____

For Thought and Discussion: In Old Testament context, Nehemiah was not wishing eternal damnation upon his enemies in 4:4-5. Rather, he was begging God not to excuse their conduct but to bring its consequences upon them in this world. What do you think of his strong language? Was he failing to love his enemies?

53

For Further Study:
Write each of your
summaries from ques-
tion 14 in your chart on
pages 34-35.

**For Thought and
Discussion:** What do
you learn from chap-
ters 3 and 4 about how
God works in the
world?

motive (verse 14) _____

_____

_____

13. Nehemiah gave two reasons for the plot's failure
    (verse 15). Name each.

    a. _____

    _____

    b. _____

    _____

14. In a sentence each, explain how you think chap-
    ters 3 and 4 reflect some of the book's themes and
    purposes.

    chapter 3 _____

    _____

    _____

    _____

    chapter 4 _____

    _____

    _____

    _____

Following the Jews' example

15. Have you discovered any principles from 4:1-23
    that apply to Christian leaders or workers? Any-
    thing about responses to opposition? If so, write
    down what you've learned and why it's important.

    _____

    _____

_____

_____

_____

_____

_____

_____

_____

For Thought and Discussion: a. Look at verses 14 and 20. How does defense based on trust in God differ from defense based on fear? (See also Judges 7, Psalm 33:16-19, Isaiah 31:1, 51:12-13.)

b. Can you think of any ways in which your nation would act differently if its people trusted God for their defense? If so, explain.

16. Do you have any other responses to 3:1-4:23—discoveries, insights, personal challenges—that are especially significant? If so, write them down here. Try to come up with one practical step that could help you begin to take what you've learned into the arena of your daily life.

_____

_____

_____

_____

_____

_____

(A vague commitment such as "I will pray more" is hard to fulfill. A specific one such as "I will pray for ten minutes before breakfast each day for courage and direction in meeting the challenge of—" is easier to fulfill.)

17. List any questions you have about these chapters.

_____

_____

_____

_____

For Further Study:
Nehemiah assumed
that his readers knew
the teaching of
Moses—Genesis
through Deuteronomy.
Study the laws of slav-
ery in Exodus 21:2-11
and Leviticus 25:39-
55. Research these
and the usury laws in
commentaries or in
R.J. Rushdoony's *Insti-
tutes of Biblical Law.*

_____

_____

_____

_____

_____

_____

The law allowed a Jew to sell himself, but the
buyer had to treat him as a servant hired for a fixed
period. The owner had to free his Jewish slave after
that period (Exodus 21:2-11, Leviticus 25:39-55,
Deuteronomy 15:12-18).

2. Behind the laws of usury and slavery were attitudes God expected them to have about one
another and about possessions. What were some
of those attitudes?

Leviticus 25:36-38 _____

_____

_____

_____

25:42 _____

_____

_____

_____

19:18 _____

_____

_____

_____

3. Why were even legal business deals out of place in
the current circumstances? What standard would
Moses (Deuteronomy 15:10-11) and Jesus (Luke
6:34,38) have applied to relationships among the
people of God when some were in need?

58

_____

_____

_____

_____

_____

_____

For Thought and Discussion: Do you think 5:1-13 offers any principles for financial interactions between Christians today? Between Christians and nonChristians? Support your answer as best you can with specifics.

4. What reason did Nehemiah give his fellow rich men to practice charity rather than strict legality (verse 9)?

_____

_____

_____

_____

5. Think how expensive it was for the rich to support the poor without interest on their loans and without knowing if they would ever get their principle back (verse 11). Yet Nehemiah condemned anyone who would not do so (verse 13). Why do you think he spoke so strongly?

_____

_____

_____

_____

6. What do you think about what Nehemiah made the rich promise to do in verse 11?

_____

_____

_____

_____

7. Is there anything you've discovered from your study of 5:1-13 that you feel God may be leading you to act on in some way? If so, write down what your response might be.

_____

_____

_____

_____

_____

_____

_____

Salary (5:14-19)

8. What was the governor's rightful salary (verses 14,18)?

_____

_____

9. Beyond that right, what did governors customarily exact from the people (verse 15)?

_____

_____

_____

_____

10. How did Nehemiah's behavior as governor differ from earlier governors' behavior (verses 16-18)?

_____

_____

_____

_____

_____

11. What two reasons did he give for his choices (verses 15,18)?

_____

_____

_____

_____

_____

_____

12. Compare his reasons with Jesus' response to a question about the greatest commandment in Mark 12:28-31. How well did Nehemiah understand the law? Explain.

_____

_____

_____

_____

_____

Following Nehemiah's example

13. Rebuilding Jerusalem's wall and people was more important to Nehemiah than getting what he had a right to. He also made his fellow Jews sacrifice their rights. Look at 1 Corinthians 9:3-18.

a. What kinds of rights do you think Christians need to sacrifice today in order to work for the building of God's Kingdom?

_____

_____

_____

61

Optional Application: Because of his practices, Nehemiah actually lost money as governor of Judah. Obeying God and aiding the people cost him. Might this attitude apply to you in any way? If you think so, explain how.

_____

_____

b. Has God called you to sacrifice any personal rights in order to live out the gospel? Why or why not?

_____

_____

_____

_____

_____

14. List any other principles for Christian living that you can find in 5:14-19.

_____

_____

_____

_____

_____

_____

15. Is there anything else you'd like to respond to or make a note of in your study of 5:14-19—perhaps a principle to apply, or an insight to take further?

_____

_____

_____

_____

_____

16. List any questions you have about chapter 5.

_____

_____

_____

_____

_____

For Further Study:
Write in your chart
(pages 34-35) how
you think chapter 5
reflects the book's
themes and purposes.

For the group

The leader or someone else should come prepared to
clarify the laws of lending and slavery (questions 1 and
2). A Bible dictionary or handbook, commentaries on
Exodus, Leviticus, Deuteronomy, or Nehemiah, and
R.J. Rushdoony's *Institutes* (see page 127) would all be
useful.

Once you all understand what the law was, discuss how the values behind it apply to Christians.
Then see how your lives in particular might better
reflect Nehemiah's attitudes.

Pray together about your decisions for application. Then hold one another accountable for those
decisions, and help each other in whatever creative
ways you can.

The Wall

Dr. Werner Keller points out the impossibility of
building a whole wall in fifty-two days (6:15). The
foundations and a great deal of broken stone were
already there. Still, the repairs necessary from the
conditions of 2:13 were drastic, and time pressed.
The British archaeologist J. Garrow Duncan describes the remains of the wall he found as follows:

"The stones are small, rough, irregular and
unequal. Some of them are unusually small and
seem to be merely chips broken off from bigger
stones, just as if they were using any kind of material that came to hand. The large holes and hollow
spaces are filled up with a haphazard mixture of
clay plaster mixed with tiny chips of stone. . . ."[1]

---

1. Werner Keller, *The Bible as History*, translated by William Neil
   (New York: William Morrow and Company, 1956 [1909]), page
   317.

63

NEHEMIAH 6:1-19

More Temptations

Read through chapter 6 a couple of times before
beginning the questions. How else can you prepare to
study in context?

The fourth challenge: negotiation
(6:1-9)

According to verse 1, the building project was in its
most critical phase. As Kidner observes, "the open
gateways . . .were the enemy's last hope of regaining
the upper hand without actually mounting a siege,
which would be out of the question against fellow subjects of Persia."[1]

The plain of Ono (verse 2) appeared to be neutral terri-
tory, halfway between Samaria and Jerusalem.
However, at nineteen miles away it was more than
a day's journey for Nehemiah. It offered him no
protection against attack from nearby unfriendly
districts, and the trip would have led him away
from his post for several crucial days. (See map on
page 37.)

---

1. Explain what you think the scheme of verse 2 was.

   _____

   _____

_____

_____

_____

2. After four rejections, the enemies were getting desperate. How did they try to frighten Nehemiah into meeting with them (verses 5-7)?

_____

_____

_____

_____

3. Why do you think Sanballat sent his message in "an unsealed letter" (verse 5)?

_____

_____

_____

_____

4. What clues told Nehemiah that the invitation to confer was an attempt to frighten him into abandoning the walls (verses 5-7,9; compare 4:1,7-8)?

_____

_____

_____

_____

5. How did Nehemiah get the courage to continue his work in the face of the threat (verse 9; compare 1:4-5,8-10)?

_____

_____

Optional Application: Could you in any way cultivate the traits or follow the principles you listed in question 6? If so, describe how you might go about it. (See for Instance Hebrews 4:12 and 5:14.)

6. What do Nehemiah's responses to subtle (verses 2-3) and threatening (verses 5-8) distractions reveal about him? Describe any character traits or principles of leadership you can glean from these incidents.

_____

_____

_____

_____

_____

_____

The fifth challenge: temptation to sin
(6:10-14)

Shut in: (verse 10). The prophet may have been staying home because of some ritual uncleanness (see Numbers 19:11-12). It could not have been a very serious one, since he would soon be free to go to the Temple.

7. Shemaiah's warning was written in Hebrew poetic verse, as was usual with prophecy. What was the warning? What was he trying to convince Nehemiah to do (verse 10)?

_____

_____

_____

_____

For Thought and Discussion: How can a Christian distinguish between warnings from God and warnings from mistaken or deceptive humans?

8. In verse 11, Nehemiah gave two responses in refusing Shemaiah. What do his responses reveal about his character?

_____

_____

_____

_____

_____

9. What do you think Nehemiah's enemies hoped to gain through the false prophecy? What would have happened if Nehemiah had given in to fear?

_____

_____

_____

_____

_____

10. How do you think Nehemiah knew that the warning was not sincere?

_____

_____

_____

_____

_____

11. What do you learn about Nehemiah from the incident with Shemaiah that is significant to you?

_____

_____

_____

_____

_____

_____

The walls completed (6:15-19)

_____

Elul: (verse 15). August-September, six months after
Nehemiah first appealed to the king.
_____

12. What was the result of Sanballat's attempt to dis-
credit Nehemiah by publicizing his work through-
out the province (see 4:2 and 6:5-7)? (Who got the
glory—verse 16?)

_____

_____

_____

_____

_____

Under oath: (verse 18). Probably trading contracts.
Tobiah, his son, and his wife's family were all
Jews. He was apparently connected with influential Jews by both marriage (to a priestly family; see
13:4) and business.
_____

13. List any principles for Christian life that you can
discover from 6:15-19.

_____

_____

_____

_____

_____

_____

_____

For Further Study:
Compare Nehemiah
6:16 to Philippians
1:12-19. Summarize
what you feel is a
godly response to pub-
lic slander or
persecution.

**For Thought and
Discussion:** *Sheca-
niah son of Arah* (verse
18) was descended
from those who
returned with Zerub-
babel (Ezra 2:5).
Tobiah was also con-
nected with the high
priest (Nehemiah
13:4). Thus, professing
Jews were undermin-
ing Nehemiah's work.
How do you think
a Christian should
respond when people
in high places who pro-
fess to be servants of
God seem to be
undermining the work
of other servants of
God? (Scripture is full
of relevant counsel.
See, for instance, Mat-
thew 7:1-5,15-20;
18:15-17; Romans
14:1; 15:1-2.)

14. How does chapter 6 reflect the themes and purposes of the book? (If you have been filling in a chart of some theme, summarize your answer there.)

_____

_____

_____

_____

15. Review the principles and lessons you found in chapter 6. Do you feel that God might be leading you to take any action or seek any change in attitude in light of 6:1-19? If so, describe here how you could respond.

_____

_____

_____

_____

_____

_____

16. List any questions you have about chapter 6.

_____

_____

_____

_____

For the group

How can you help one another to resist temptations like those Nehemiah faced? To discern whether counsel is from God or the enemy? To acquire the qualities you described in questions 6, 13, and 15? Discuss any specific dilemmas that group members may be facing.

1. Kidner, page 98.

NEHEMIAH 7:1-8:6

The City Put to Use

Prepare for study as you normally do. Try not to get bogged down in chapter 7, but look for the overall purpose of the chapter. Also, be alert for details that you either find important or do not understand.

The holy city (7:1-3)

The gatekeepers and the singers and the Levites: (verse 1). Some gatekeepers guarded the city gates; others guarded the holy place and its valuables. The singers performed the music and choral prayers for temple worship. The Levites each had assigned tasks for temple upkeep.

1. The building project was not an end in itself, but a means to something further. What does the appointment of gatekeepers, singers, and Levites (verse 1) tell you about the purpose of the city?

   _____

   _____

   _____

   _____

   _____

Why do you think Nehemiah wanted to know the ancestry of everyone who claimed to be a Jew? Why was the connection to Israel before the exile so important to the problem of repopulating Jerusalem? (See 2:20; see also the basis of a claim to be one of God's holy people in Genesis 17:8.)

2. Does the purpose of the holy city suggest anything about God's purposes for His holy nation today? (Compare Ephesians 1:5-6, 1 Peter 2:9.)

_____

_____

_____

_____

_____

The holy people (7:4-72)

3. What was the record that Nehemiah copied into 7:6-72 (verses 5-7)?

_____

_____

_____

_____

The temple servants: (verse 46) and *the descendants of the servants of Solomon* (verse 57). David created a corps of assistants to the Levites to take some of the more menial tasks of temple upkeep. Solomon evidently added a further group of assistants. Some of these men seem to have been descended from converts to the worship of the Lord in David's day, since the list includes non-Hebrew names (they are family names, not first names). At least at that time, purity of ancestry had been less important than a sincere commitment to God's commands, including circumcision.

Urim and Thummim: (verse 65). Objects placed in or on the high priest's breastpiece (Exodus 28:30). The method is debated, but somehow they were used to discern God's will. Some scholars have guessed that they were lots. At any rate, they were used in David's time but missing by Nehemiah's.

---

4. What do you learn about God from the fact that He gave His promises to a family, and that one could claim His promises only by being accepted into the family?

_____

_____

_____

_____

_____

_____

Holy words (7:73-8:6)

The seventh month: (7:73). The month immediately after the wall was finished. The first day of the month was the Feast of Trumpets (Rosh Hashanah). In the twentieth century, this feast marks the beginning of a new civil year, while the religious year changes at Passover, but in Nehemiah's day the religious year was the only one. For more on the feast, see Leviticus 23:24-25.

In their towns: (7:73). Few people lived in Jerusalem (see 7:4,73); most lived in villages a day or more distant. However, the Law required that all Jews assemble in Jerusalem on the Feast of Trumpets.

---

5. a. What event was planned for the festival assembly (8:1)?

_____

_____

_____

b. Who requested this event?

_____

_____

73

Assembly: (verse 2). In the Greek Old Testament which Jews of Jesus' day used, the Hebrew word for "assembly" was translated *ekklesia.* Paul used this word in his letters frequently; it is translated into English as "church."

6. Who attended the reading (verse 2)?

_____

_____

_____

_____

7. Notice the behavior of the people in verses 3 and 5-6. What do you think motivated their response?

_____

_____

_____

_____

_____

_____

8. Do you think the people's attitude toward God's Word was a necessary first step toward a revival of allegiance to God? Why or why not?

_____

_____

_____

_____

_____

9. List any insights for today that you found in 7:1-8:6.

_____

_____

_____

_____

_____

_____

_____

10. List any questions you have about 7:1-8:6.

_____

_____

_____

_____

_____

_____

Optional Application: According to one view of the book's purpose, everything that has happened so far is building up to a revival of faith and godliness in Judah. One theme is, "How does a revival happen?" In preceding questions you may have been noting what led up to this revival— the attitudes and choices of God, a leader, and a group of people.

Do the events in Nehemiah's book suggest any ways that the Church today might cooperate with God in reviving faith and obedience? How might you participate?

Keep noticing the process of revival in the following chapters.

For the group

How to foster revival might be a good focus for your discussion. You could let the other questions lead to this application.

Continue to share what principles you found and how you are applying them to your lives. Keep encouraging each other to persevere with past applications.

NEHEMIAH 8:7-18

Revival

Read 8:7-18 several times, and recall the context of where the story is moving. Do you have a sense of how chapter 8 fits the book's themes?

God's Word understood (8:7-12)

The Levites: (verse 7). According to RSV and NIV, the thirteen men in verse 7 *were* the Levites who moved through the crowd while fourteen men on the platform were reading (verse 4). According to NASB and KJV, the thirteen in verse 7 were *additional to* the Levites who also moved through the crowd.

Making it clear: (verse 8). The NIV suggests that the people understood the Hebrew language being read but needed explanation. The teachers explained the reading section by section. NASB says the teachers were *translating* the reading; NASB assumes that the hearers knew only the Aramaic language. NASB gives *explaining* as an alternate reading.

---

1. Why do you think the people responded to what they heard as they did in verse 9? (We don't know exactly what they heard, but the Law describes

what God had done for Israel and what He
expected of Israel.)

_____

_____

_____

_____

_____

_____

2. a. What did Nehemiah tell the people to do
   instead of their first reaction (verses 9-10)?

_____

_____

_____

_____

   b. What reasons did he give (verses 9-10)?

_____

_____

_____

_____

_____

3. From verses 9-10, explain in your own words why
   celebration was a better response to the Law than
   grief.

_____

_____

_____

_____

_____

_____

4. Nehemiah said to celebrate because "This day is sacred [holy] to our Lord" (verse 10).

   a. Why do you think Nehemiah declared it a holy day?

   _____

   _____

   _____

   _____

   _____

   b. What do you think the day's *holiness* had to do with celebration vs. mourning?

   _____

   _____

   _____

   _____

   _____

5. Nehemiah told the people to share their feasts with those who could not make any, such as the elderly, poor, and widowed (verse 10). This was what God commanded the Israelites to do when they celebrated God's fulfillment of His promises (see Deuteronomy 26:5-15).

   What attitudes (about the source and purpose of their possessions, about the poor among them, etc.) did sharing show?

   _____

   _____

   _____

   _____

   _____

79

Optional Application: Imagine that Christians have been unable to celebrate Easter for seventy years, and that no one has had Bibles in which to read about Jesus. At last circumstances have changed—Bibles are available, and an Easter celebration is planned. Describe the atmosphere of that celebration. (Also, consider the implications of this scenario for your own attitudes and actions right now.)

6. What do you think "the joy of the LORD" (verse 10) is, and why is it our strength?

_____

_____

_____

_____

_____

_____

_____

7. "Understanding" (verses 2,3,8,12) describes a thorough grasp of the reading's meaning. It goes beyond just knowing what the text says. Why do you think understanding was so important to the revival that Nehemiah kept repeating the word?

_____

_____

_____

_____

_____

_____

8. a. Why do you think the people responded first in grief, then in joy, once they had heard and understood God's Word?

_____

_____

_____

_____

_____

_____

80

b. How might this progression relate to response to the gospel today?

_____

_____

_____

_____

_____

_____

9. Review 8:1-12, and list the first elements of spiritual revival described there.

_____

_____

_____

_____

_____

_____

_____

_____

10. Name any other principles for Christian practice that you think 8:1-12 teaches.

_____

_____

_____

_____

_____

_____

Optional Application: Can you think of any action you might take to encourage or sustain a revival in your own devotion to God? If so, describe that action.

Optional Application: Is there anything you could do to encourage revival in another person, your church, or your community? How might you accomplish this goal?

The Feast of Booths (8:13-18)

11. On the day after this revival, some of the people met with Ezra for detailed study of the Law. Who were those people (verse 13)?

_____

_____

12. Why did these people meet to study Torah? (See Deuteronomy 6:6-7.)

_____

_____

_____

_____

Booths: (verse 14). The Feast of Trumpets was the first day of the month. The tenth day was the Day of Atonement (Yom Kippur), another day of rest for repentance from the year's sins. Nehemiah did not mention that holy day, perhaps because it did not require the people to gather in Jerusalem and so did not figure in the main thread of his story. The dramatic events occurred when the people came together. (For more on the Day of Atonement, see Leviticus 16:[6-28]29-31; 23:27-32.)

The Feast of Booths, or Tabernacles (Leviticus 23:34-36,39-43), lasted for eight days, beginning on the fifteenth of the month. The booths were tents like those in which the Israelites lived while they wandered with Moses. The booths were meant to remind the Jews of that pilgrimage—of their ancestors' miraculous deliverance from slavery and of God's care for them in the desert.

---

13. Describe how the Jews celebrated the Feast of Booths (Nehemiah 8:15-18).

_____

_____

_____

_____

_____

Optional Application: Christians celebrate certain great acts of God in their history, such as Easter. How could the the Jews' attitudes, shown in chapter 8, enrich a Christian celebration?

14. a. Imagine being a Jewish farmer or craftsman celebrating the Feast of Booths. You would never in your life have lived in a nomad's tent. How do you think it would have felt to live for a week in a tent of branches on a city rooftop?

_____

_____

_____

b. How do you think your own or your parents' experience of release from exile in Babylon would have affected your understanding of the Exodus, and vice versa?

_____

_____

_____

_____

_____

15. The Feast of Booths was also a harvest festival, like Thanksgiving (Leviticus 23:39). For what would the Jews have been giving thanks in that year?

_____

_____

_____

_____

_____

_____

Optional Application: Meditate daily for the next week on Nehemiah 8:10. Think about what it meant to the Jews in their situation, and what it means to you.

Optional Application: Pray for ways to begin living verses 10 and 12. How might a group of Christians (a Bible study, a church, etc.) help each other to celebrate holiness and God's Word with joy?

16. List any other principles you believe 8:13-18 offers to Christians today.

_____

_____

_____

_____

_____

_____

_____

17. How do chapters 7 and 8 relate to the themes and purposes of the book? (If you're keeping a chart, write in it how these chapters reflect the theme you are following.)

_____

_____

_____

_____

_____

_____

18. List any questions you have about 8:7-18.

_____

_____

_____

_____

For the group

Questions 1, 3, and 9 are central to this passage. Once you have grasped them, you could discuss applications. Consider praying together for discernment in applying the passage to your lives.

NEHEMIAH 9:1-37

Confession

You may want to review chapter 8 when you read chapter 9. Recall the people's first mood (8:9) and second mood (8:12), and observe their mood in chapter 9.

 The last day of the Feast of Booths was the twenty-second of the month, when the people were rejoicing in thanks for deliverance, the law, and the city. Two days later, they assembled as 9:1 describes.

1. Why do you think the Jews assembled fasting, wearing sackcloth, and with dust on their heads (verse 1)?

  _____

  _____

  _____

  _____

  _____

  _____

  _____

Separated themselves from all foreigners (verse 2) does not necessarily mean that they divorced and broke social relations with everyone who lacked pure Jewish blood. These thoughts will be pursued in later lessons; see 10:30 and 13:3.

2. "A fourth of the day" (verse 3) was about three hours. What two things did the Jews do on this day for three hours each (verses 2-3)?

_____

_____

_____

Called: (verse 4). NASB and RSV read "cried." The word implies sorrow.

---

3. The sorrowful cry (verse 4) led into the song (verses 5-37). The song included worship (verses 5-8) and confession (verses 33-35). How are worship and confession—praise and sorrow—related?

_____

_____

_____

_____

_____

4. Verses 5 through 37 are a song of praise. In the chart below, summarize what each stanza says about God—about His character and what He has done. (The divisions are the paragraphs in the NIV. Feel free to change them if your Bible differs.)

God's Acts	God's Character
verses 5-6	

God's Acts	God's Character
verses 7-8	
verses 9-12	
verses 13-15	
verses 16-18	

God's Acts	God's Character
verses 19-21	
verses 22-25	
verses 26-31	
verses 32-37	

5. God responded to Israel's disobedience in two ways. Name each way. (Think about how each reflected His compassion.)

a. (verses 18-21) _____

_____

_____

_____

b. (verses 26-27) _____

_____

_____

_____

For Thought and Discussion: Look at your answer to question 6. Can you find any principles there for confession?

6. a. What did the Jews blame for their misfortunes (verses 33 37)?

_____

_____

b. What was their view of how God had treated them (verse 33)?

_____

_____

_____

_____

7. Below are two sets of sentences. In each set, choose the one that you think agrees with chapter 9.

a. (verse 27)
☐ God saved the Jews time after time because He was compassionate, even though they deserved their misfortunes.
☐ The Jews earned deliverance from Egypt and from later oppressors by obedience to God.

For Thought and Discussion: Verse 29 makes the statement that a man will live if he obeys God's commandments. Do you think this statement should be taken literally? Why or why not? What kind of "life" is referred to here?

b. (verses 16-20,29-30)
☐ God considers obedience to His rules to be more important than a relationship of trust.
☐ God considers a relationship of trust to be more important than obedience to His rules.
☐ God desires that we show our relationship of trust by obeying His rules.

8. a. God rescued His people from oppression each time after they did something. What did they do that brought about this response from God (verses 27-28)?

_____

_____

_____

_____

b. How might this principle apply to Christians today?

_____

_____

_____

_____

_____

_____

9. What was the role of "grace" (undeserved kindness) in the Jews' beliefs? (See, for instance, verses 7-8,17,20,31-32.)

_____

_____

_____

_____

_____

_____

_____

_____

10. For this rare moment in their history, the Jews had joy and penitent obedience in healthy balance. What views of God or self might lead a person to overemphasize joy or penitence?

_____

_____

_____

_____

_____

_____

For Thought and Discussion: The Jews followed a joyous re-experience of God's love (chapter 8) with a repentant recommitment to obedience (chapter 9). Is this ever important for Christians? Why or why not?

For Further Study: Explain how chapter 9 witnesses to both God's justice and His mercy.

11. How does chapter 9 contribute to the theme of the book of Nehemiah? (If you are keeping a chart, summarize your answer there.)

_____

_____

_____

_____

_____

Looking at your own life

12. Study the sequence of events in verses 25 through 31. What can you discover about human nature and God from those events?

human nature _____

_____

_____

_____

God _____

_____

_____

_____

_____

13. a. What are some of the methods that God might use to make us aware when we take His gifts for granted, take credit for our success, or for some other reason stop listening to Him?

_____

_____

_____

_____

_____

_____

b. Describe two or three possible ways of responding to being made aware of ingratitude or disobedience.

_____

_____

_____

_____

_____

_____

c. How can we learn to respond properly?

_____

_____

_____

_____

_____

_____

14. List any other lessons from chapter 9 that you think are relevant today.

Optional Application: Are there any lessons about prayer in chapter 9 that you might apply to your own prayer life? If so, what are they?

_____

_____

_____

_____

_____

_____

_____

15. Record here any other responses you've had to chapter 9 that you would like to act on in the coming week.

_____

_____

_____

_____

_____

_____

16. List any questions you have about chapter 9.

_____

_____

_____

_____

_____

For the group

Let each person share some of his observations about the prayer of confession. Ask if anyone would like to share with the group at least one way he is applying an observation to himself. You might also discuss how your private and group prayer has affected your attitudes and decisions over the last few weeks.

LESSON ELEVEN

NEHEMIAH 9:38-10:31

Recommitment

Read 9:38-10:31. Don't get bogged down in the names (10:2 27), but do observe details from the rest of the passage. Keep the book's themes in mind.

If your time is limited you could study only one or two of the four laws in 10:30-31.

1. The "binding agreement" of 10:1-39 was among the whole people—leaders, temple workers, and every layperson "able to understand" (10:28). What did they agree to do (10:29)?

_____

_____

_____

_____

2. Verse 9:38 says that the agreement was made *because* of the confession and prayer of 9:5-37. Why do you think it was crucial that this agreement followed that prayer?

_____

_____

_____

_____

_____

For Further Study:
The agreement singled out several laws for explicit mention (10:30-31). Why do you think these particular laws were chosen?

For Thought and
Discussion: What do
you think was God's
purpose in limiting the
Jews' contact and
involvement with
non-Jews?

Mixed marriage (10:30)

3. Read the following references, and name the reasons God gave for prohibiting alliances with polytheists (those who worship many gods).

Exodus 34:12-16 _____

_____

_____

_____

_____

Leviticus 20:26 _____

_____

_____

_____

_____

1 Kings 11:1-4 _____

_____

_____

_____

4. Ruth, the great-grandmother of King David, was from Moab. However, before she went to Judah she promised to worship the Lord alone (Ruth 1:16). The Old Testament records other examples of converts welcomed into the nation (see the comment on 7:46,57 on page 72). From this information and from question 3, choose the completion that makes this sentence true: A Jew could marry and form alliances . . .

☐ only with someone of pure Jewish blood.
☐ only with someone committed to worshiping the Lord alone according to His commands.
☐ only with someone of pure Jewish blood who was also committed to worshiping the Lord alone according to His commands.
☐ with anyone he chose.

5. Look at 2 Corinthians 6:14-7:1. Why did Paul command Christians not to marry pagans?

_____

_____

_____

_____

_____

_____

_____

The Sabbath day (10:31)

6. The Law forbade Jews from working or causing anyone to work on the Sabbath, and it was work to buy from pagans. Read Exodus 20:8-11 and Deuteronomy 5:12-15. Why were the Jews supposed to keep the Sabbath *holy*?

_____

_____

_____

_____

The sabbath year (10:31)

Forgo working the land: (verse 31). According to Exodus 23:10-11, there was to be a year of rest from farming as there was a day of rest in the week. The reason given was so that poor people and wild animals could take whatever they wanted from the fallow fields. The Jews may or may not have known that leaving a field fallow for a year keeps it

For Further Study: On the other hand, Christ ate and stayed with immoral Jews and pagans. So did His apostles. What do you think holiness (separation) means for a Christian, who is commissioned to bring the gospel to unbelievers? Think of as many principles as you can. (If you like, see Matthew 15:10-11, 17-20; Luke 5:27-32; 10:30-37; 14:12-14; 1 Corinthians 5:9-13; Ephesians 5:11.)

For Thought and Discussion: Christians are not bound to keep the Jewish law. However, do you think the Sabbath offers any principles for a Christian lifestyle? Support your answer with Scripture references, if you can.

97

For Thought and Discussion: Do you think these values, attitudes, or practices of the sabbath year offer any principles for Christians today? Why or why not?

more fertile by allowing nutrients in the soil to replenish themselves.

According to 2 Chronicles 36:20-21, God ordained 70 years of captivity because the people had neglected seventh-year sabbaths for 490 years (ca. 1095-605 BC). The land was owed 70 missed years of rest.

7. Read Leviticus 25:4-7,20-22. How did God promise to provide food when no one planted?

_____

_____

_____

_____

_____

8. The sabbath year seemed to endanger profits. But what fact were the people to keep in mind when they used natural resources (Leviticus 25:23)?

_____

_____

_____

_____

_____

9. What does this law reveal about God's concern for living things—human, animal, and plant?

_____

_____

_____

_____

_____

10. Describe the attitude toward God you think a person would need to have to forgo planting for a year on the strength of His promise.

_____

_____

_____

_____

_____

For Thought and Discussion: Do you think the law of suspending/canceling debts teaches any values, attitudes, or practices for Christians today? If so, what? If not, why not?

Cancel all debts: (verse 31). In the same sabbatical year, everyone who had loaned money to another Jew was to release him from that debt.[1]

11. In Deuteronomy 15:4-6, God promised that a lender could afford to forgo collecting on debts every seven years even though he would have no income from land in that year. According to God, why could he afford this?

_____

_____

_____

_____

_____

12. What attitudes about giving did God command and condemn (Deuteronomy 15:7-11)?

Command	Condemn

99

13. List any questions you have about 9:38-10:31.

_____

_____

_____

_____

_____

_____

_____

For the group

The laws of the sabbatical year are controversial—people disagree on what principles they teach and on how they apply to Christians. Some people think all Old Testament laws are obsolete since Christ came; others think the laws reflect timeless principles of justice even though keeping them does not earn God's acceptance. Try to consider each member's views with discernment and without scorn. Pray for discernment before you discuss.

You may decide to skip questions 4-5 or take two meetings for the lesson. Or, you may want to study just one or two of the laws. Perhaps someone in the group should research in commentaries the laws you do study.

1. Scholars agree that _release_ meant at least that nothing was due during that year, for a man paid his debts from the produce of his land. Kidner (page 116; compare J.A. Thompson, _Deuteronomy_ [Downers Grove, Illinois: InterVarsity Press, 1974], pages 185-188) thinks it also meant that the debt was permanently canceled. Peter Craigie and others (Peter C. Craigie, _The Book of Deuteronomy_ [Grand Rapids, Michigan: William B. Eerdmans Publishing Company, 1976], pages 237-238; C.F. Karl and Franz Delitzsche, _Commentary on the Old Testament: Volume I: The Pentateuch_ [Grand Rapids, Michigan: William B. Eerdmans Publishing Company, 1976], part III, pages 369-370) think that _release_ meant postponement, not permanent cancellation, since cancellation would have upset people's legitimate property rights. NIV translates "will cancel all debts," whereas NASB reads "will forego. . .the exaction of every debt." See Deuteronomy 15:1-3.

100

NEHEMIAH 10:32-13:3

The Holy City

Read 10:28-31 along with 10:32-13:3 before you begin to study. You can skim the names in 11:4-12:26, but notice the categories of people listed. Think about what all this has to do with the point of the story.

Paying for worship (10:32-39)

Recall the economic priorities the Jews' agreement showed in 10:30-31. These next commitments belong with those priorities.

1. The agreement went into careful detail about how each Jew was to support the worship of the Lord. The people paid for offerings; supplied wood; and supported priests, musicians, maintenance men, etc. (10:32-39).

    What attitudes toward worship do you think these provisions reflect?

    _____

    _____

    _____

    _____

    _____

    _____

    _____

For Thought and Discussion: Do you think the attitudes you noted in question 1 have any relevance to a Christian's economic priorities? Explain why or why not.

For Further Study:
Verses 12:1-26 list the high priests, priestly divisions, and Levites from the first return of exiles in 538 BC (verse 1) until Nehemiah's time. Why do you think the family continuity of priests and Levites over a century was important enough to include? (See Numbers 3:9-13, especially verse 10.)

Populating Jerusalem (11:1-12:26)

2. Recall from 7:4 that few people lived in Jerusalem. Name the two ways in which the Jews made sure that "the holy city" was repopulated with believers (11:1).

_____

_____

_____

_____

_____

3. Why do you think Nehemiah felt it was important to have certain people living in Jerusalem?

_____

_____

_____

_____

_____

The wall is dedicated (12:27-47)

Since 7:5, Nehemiah's memoirs have given way to documents from the temple archives and to narration by the book's editor. Now we return to Nehemiah's voice for the rest of the book. The dedication of the new walls probably occurred shortly after the events of chapters 8 through 10.

4. What was to be the chief way of celebrating the dedication (12:27)?

_____

_____

_____

_____

102

5. The priests and Levites prepared for the celebration by purifying themselves, the people, the gates, and the wall (verse 30). This was probably ceremonial washing. Why do you think everyone and everything needed to be washed (see Leviticus 11:44-45, Numbers 8:21)?

_____

_____

_____

_____

_____

For Thought and Discussion: Does verse 30 suggest to you any principles for a Christian's life or worship? Name those principles, or explain why you think the verse is no longer relevant.

Routes of the Two Processions

"We cannot be quite certain," says Kidner,[1] but like Nehemiah in 2:13, they probably started at the Valley Gate on the west side. (See the map on page 40.) Ezra's procession went counter-clockwise and Nehemiah's clockwise, and both met at the Temple. ("Right"—verse 31—and "left"—verse 38—are relative to one standing facing the city from outside or on top of the west wall.) Kidner arranges the two processions as follows:[2]

Group led by Ezra, toward the right:
Thanksgiving choir
Hoshaiah
"Half of the princes"
Priests with trumpets (seven of them named,
    Azariah to Jeremiah)
Instrumentalists
(Zechariah and eight others)

Group proceeding toward the left:
Thanksgiving choir
Nehemiah
"Half of the officials"
Priests with trumpets (seven named, from Eliakim
    to Hananiah)
Singers
(Jezrahiah and eight others)

Choirs: (verses 31,38,40). This word translates a single Hebrew word meaning "thanksgivings" or "confessions."[3] In other words, these choirs embodied what they sang, as each "thanksgiving" marched in a different direction and met at last at the Temple.

6. What did the two choirs do (verses 31,37-40)?

_____

_____

_____

_____

_____

_____

7. Summarize how the Jews celebrated (verses 27,35,42-43).

_____

_____

_____

_____

_____

8. Compare the procession and celebration of the wall to Psalm 48:11-14. Besides thanking God for what He had done and praising Him for who He is, what were other purposes of such a procession?

_____

_____

_____

_____

_____

_____

This celebration was a very special occasion; ordinary worship would not have been so elaborate. Nevertheless, the account gives a sense of how Jews liked to worship their God.

More notes on worship (12:44-47)

After the dedication, the Jews were evidently all enthusiastic about supporting Jerusalem worship. Even people who were not wealthy had to pay for professional musicians, priests, and temple workers. The priests and Levites were the nation's only civil service and performed many duties; nevertheless, much of the money supported worship services.

9. Why do you think all this effort and expense for worship was important to the Jews?

_____

_____

_____

_____

_____

For Thought and Discussion: Do you think Judah's effort and expense for worship offer any principles for Christians? (For instance, would such expense be acceptable today?) Why or why not?

Separation—again (13:1-3)

Verses 1 and 2 summarize Deuteronomy 23:3-5. The prohibition seems harsh, even chauvinistic, but remember the purpose of this rule from lesson eleven, questions 3-5.

10. Lessons ten through twelve of this study guide break 9:1-13:3 rather arbitrarily. Recognizing that the following divisions are also arbitrary, tell how you think each reflects some of the themes of the book.

9:1-38 _____

_____

_____

_____

For Further Study:
Write these four sum-
maries into your chart.

**Optional
Application:** Have you
made any personal
discoveries in your
study of Nehemiah
10:32-13:3 that call
for some kind of action
on your part? If so,
describe how you
could respond.

10:1-39 _____

_____

_____

11:1-12:26 _____

_____

_____

_____

12:27-13:3 _____

_____

_____

_____

11. List any questions you have about this lesson.

_____

_____

_____

_____

_____

_____

For the group

If you want to cover the book of Nehemiah more
quickly, you could omit this lesson. However, the
issue of attitudes about worship services could spark a
fruitful discussion.

1. Kidner, page 126.
2. Kidner, page 127.
3. Kidner, page 126.

NEHEMIAH 13:4-22

Nehemiah Leaves and Returns

Prepare for studying this passage as you usually do.

Infiltration (13:4-9)

Recall that shortly after the dedication of the wall, in his first year as governor, Nehemiah had seen to it that honest men were put in charge of the valuable temple furnishings and of the stores which supported the temple worship (12:44). Eliashib, as high priest, had been made the top man in charge. For twelve years, while Nehemiah had been governor, everything had apparently been done honestly. But in 433 BC Nehemiah had returned to Persia (13:6). Then, after some unspecified time, he had been reappointed governor of Judah (13:6-7). During his absence, some of the zeal of the Jews' spiritual revival had cooled, and abuses had crept in.

1. "Closely associated with" (NASB: "related to"; verse 4) may or may not imply family connection. What had Eliashib done for Tobiah (verse 5)?

   _____

   _____

   _____

   _____

   _____

For Thought and Discussion: Can you discover anything about spiritual revival from 13:4-9? If so, what?

2. Why do you think Tobiah wanted to live in a temple storeroom? (Think about what a base in the Temple situated him to do.)

_____
_____
_____
_____
_____

3. Explain why Eliashib's act was severe sin (verse 7).

_____
_____
_____
_____
_____

4. What do you learn about Nehemiah from his response when he returned from Persia (verses 8-9)?

_____
_____
_____
_____
_____
_____

5. Why do you think the other Jews did not take this action while Nehemiah was away?

_____
_____
_____
_____

6. What principles about biblical leadership can you learn from 13:4-9?

_____

_____

_____

_____

_____

_____

_____

7. Does this passage offer any other lessons for Christians? List any you can find.

_____

_____

_____

_____

_____

_____

For Thought and Discussion: a. Think through a current issue (regarding morals, public policy, etc.) on which you think Christians should take a stand. What are some reasons why Christians might avoid taking the kind of firm action Nehemiah exhibited in this passage to support such a stand?

b. What do you think proper Christian action in response to this issue might be? (Every person will not act identically, but you might suggest some possibilities.)

Paying for worship (13:10-14)

8. Describe the next sign of decay that Nehemiah found on his return (verse 10).

_____

_____

_____

9. What attitudes toward worship and financial priorities does this change in behavior suggest? (Look back at question 1 of lesson twelve.)

_____

_____

For Further Study: Do you think the principle of tithing applies to Christians? If so, how and why? If not, why not? (See Matthew 23:23; 1 Corinthians 9:7,14; Philippians 4:15-19.)

10. What further principles of leadership or obedience do you learn from Nehemiah's response to this lapse (verses 11,13)?

_____

_____

_____

_____

_____

_____

The Sabbath (13:15-22)

11. What was the third abuse that Nehemiah discovered on his return (verses 15-16)?

_____

_____

_____

12. Observe the measures he took to put an end to this abuse (verses 19-22). What new traits of a leader or principles of leadership can you find in this response?

_____

_____

_____

110

_____

_____

_____

13. Review what you wrote in questions 6-12 of lesson eleven about the Jews' attitude toward the Sabbath. Describe below the changes in the Jews' attitudes that you think the disregard of the Sabbath showed.

Attitude	Change
toward God's ability to provide for their needs	
toward their ability to provide for themselves without God	
toward the day set aside to honor God	

14. a. Since the Jews had ceased to support public worship and to rest on the Sabbath, do you

For Further Study:
Nehemiah feared that God would punish the sin of 13:15-16 as He had punished it before (verse 18). He was thinking of the words of Jeremiah, who prophesied to Judah just before Babylon crushed her. Read Jeremiah 17:19-27. Why do you think Sabbath-breaking was so serious?

think they were still leaving their fields fallow
every seven years, waiving debts, and caring for
the needy?

_____

_____

_____

b. Explain your answer by describing how you expect
that the following attitudes had or had not
changed.

Area	Attitude
the source of wealth	
the right to control one's pos-sessions	
poverty and poor people	

112

15. Has your study of 13:4-22 brought to light any specific application that you feel led to make? Jot it down here, and then pray about how it might help deepen your walk with God.

For Thought and Discussion: How do you decide what relevance, if any, Old Testament commands like keeping a holy place, tithing, the Sabbath, and notions of ownership and sharing have for modern Christians?

_____

_____

_____

_____

_____

_____

_____

16. List any questions you have about this passage.

_____

_____

_____

_____

_____

For the group

You may want to focus your discussion on just one of the three abuses, exploring what it implied at the time and what principles for Christians it suggests. Examine Nehemiah's character as well. If you decide ahead of time, group members may come well prepared for a specific topic.

NEHEMIAH 13:23-31 AND REVIEW

Looking Back

Your review will be most fruitful if you reread the whole book. That may sound like a lot of work, but you'll find that the results will go a long way in helping you retain a thorough grasp of the book. Look again for themes, the story's movement, actions of major characters, and clues to the author's purpose.

If rereading the whole book seems impossible, even skimming important sections of the book, reading your chart (if you kept one), and thinking through this study guide will probably help you remember the book fairly well.

Intermarriage—again (13:23-30)

This paragraph connects closely with 13:3-22.

1. The fourth lapse that the Jews committed in Nehemiah's absence was intermarriage with the very pagans from whom they had three times (9:2, 10:30, and 13:3) promised to separate. What effect on the children of those mixed marriages particularly dismayed Nehemiah (verse 24)?

_____

_____

_____

_____

For Thought and Discussion: Observe how Nehemiah treated the men who had taken foreign wives (verse 25). Why do you suppose he reacted like this?

2. Remember the reason why God prohibited such marriages (see, for instance, verse 26). Why was this effect on the children so serious? That is, why do you think it was crucial for Jewish children to speak Hebrew?

_____

_____

_____

_____

_____

3. Why do you think the Jews found it so hard to keep from allying themselves with unbelievers?

_____

_____

_____

_____

_____

4. The Jews had sworn to avoid each of the sins into which they fell while Nehemiah was away (10:28-39). Some (chiefly intermarriage) they had struggled with repeatedly. When they rededicated themselves yet again during Nehemiah's second term as governor, do you think they expected God to forgive and accept them after so many failures? Why or why not?

_____

_____

_____

_____

_____

116

5. Can you discover any principles for the Christian life from the record of Nehemiah's final reforms in 13:23-31? If so, what are they?

_____

_____

_____

_____

_____

_____

_____

For Thought and Discussion: What do you think about Nehemiah's prayers that he and his enemies be remembered for their deeds? (For instance, do you think he believed that he had been earning God's favor?)

For Further Study: Finish your chart by writing in its last space how 13:4-31 serves the theme of the book of Nehemiah that you are tracing.

What I have so faithfully done: (verse 14). Literally, "acts of covenant love."

---

6. a. Three times in this chapter, Nehemiah asked God to remember him and his deeds (see also 5:19). For what did he say he wanted to be remembered (13:14,22,31)?

_____

_____

_____

_____

   b. For what did he ask God to remember the corrupt priests (verse 29; compare 4:4-5 and 6:14)?

_____

_____

_____

_____

Review

7. Look back at your answers in previous lessons. What did you learn from your study about

God's plan in history _____

_____

_____

_____

_____

_____

_____

God's character _____

_____

_____

_____

_____

_____

_____

prayer _____

_____

_____

_____

_____

_____

_____

obedience _____

_____

_____

_____

_____

_____

_____

leadership _____

_____

_____

_____

_____

building God's Kingdom _____

_____

_____

_____

_____

other main lessons of the book _____

_____

_____

_____

_____

8. Would you now revise your statements of the book's main goals that you made in lesson one? If

so, explain here what you think the book's chief
purposes are.

_____

_____

_____

_____

_____

_____

9. Look back at the questions about the book that
you listed at the end of lesson one. (Also, scan
through any questions you may have noted at the
end of each study lesson.)

Has your study of the book answered these
questions? If not, do any of the questions still
seem important to you? If you do still have significant questions, consider possible ways of further
study on your own, or with someone who could
help you, in order to resolve these questions.

Following Nehemiah's example

10. Has your study of Nehemiah prompted a recogni-
tion of a specific need to pursue further growth in
some aspect of your walk with the Lord? If so,
consider how you might start and then keep
going. Selecting and memorizing one or more key
verses for this area can be a real help.

_____

_____

_____

_____

_____

_____

_____

11. You may have committed yourself to some actions during your study. Are you satisfied with your follow-through? If not, review the reasons why you made those commitments. If they still hold up, pray about how you can live obediently in response to what God asks of you.

Optional Application: a. Has your prayer life grown since you began this study? If so, what has been most significant?

b. Have you made any discoveries that you feel will help you become more sensitive to God's work in your life, more able to respond to Him in practical obedience? (If so, write it down! This is a major insight.)

_____

_____

_____

_____

_____

_____

For the group

By God's grace, you should finish your study with a grasp of the themes of Nehemiah, a sense of how you have grown individually and corporately, and a direction for further study and growth. As you discuss these, evaluate how the group functioned during your study. What would you do the same or differently? Also, identify members' current needs and decide what you might do next.

121

GOING ON IN NEHEMIAH

Now that you've completed this study guide, you might still feel that you have not yet finished with the book of Nehemiah. Perhaps you want to return to matters that you had to treat only briefly during your study. Below are some suggested ways to pursue further study of the book of Nehemiah, or to take a closer look in the rest of the Old Testament at some of the issues the book raises.

1. Recall from lesson two that Nehemiah saw himself as standing "in the breach" to save Israel through prayer. To learn more about standing in the breach, study Psalm 106:21-23; Exodus 32:7-14; Ezekiel 13:3-6, 22:30-31. What is this mission? When and why is it necessary? Who was called to it in Israel? Does God call anyone to it now?
2. Study each of Nehemiah's prayers. Notice the purpose of each, and the attitudes about self and God that each shows. Notice when, where, how, and why Nehemiah prayed. Compare the prayers of Abraham (Genesis 18:20-33), Hannah (1 Samuel 1:11, 2:1-10), Hezekiah (2 Kings 19:15-19), David, or Paul.
3. List Nehemiah's character qualities and how he exhibited each. Then compare the qualities of another leader, such as Moses, Joshua, David, Ezra, Jesus, or Paul. Or, compare how Nehemiah responded to adversity to the response of one of these leaders in a crisis.
4. Nehemiah was a trusted official in the Persian court. To learn more about the life of a Jew in Persia, study Mordecai in the book of Esther. Or, compare Daniel in the Babylonian court 150 years earlier, or Joseph in Egypt 1000 years earlier.
5. Study chapters 8 through 10 of Nehemiah to see how a revival of faith develops. Think about how a revival might occur in your church or community.
6. Study the major feasts commanded in the Old Testament. What was each supposed to remind the Israelites about God and themselves? See Exodus 12:1-28, Leviticus 23:1-44, Numbers 28:16-29:40, Deuteronomy 16:1-17.
7. Study in their original context the laws about property and priorities Nehemiah struggled to enforce. First think carefully about Deuteronomy 5:6-21, the Ten Commandments. All the other laws were applications of these to Israelite culture. Think about the implications of putting nothing before God,

of work and rest, of valuing life, of not coveting, etc.
  a. The sabbatical and jubilee years—Leviticus 25. Study Leviticus 19—27 for
     the context of how God wanted His people to order their society, and other
     values He wanted to instill. Read in a Bible almanac or encyclopedia about
     life in Palestine under Joshua and under Nehemiah. Can principles appli-
     cable then be applied in your culture?
  b. Lending money—Deuteronomy 15:1-18, 23:15-26:19. Read Deuteronomy
     4—11 for the context of how God and His people were related.
8. Study the concept of salvation in the Old Testament. Begin with the references in Nehemiah (1:9, 9:27-28). Then move to Exodus, Deuteronomy, Isaiah,
   Jeremiah, etc. Look up in a concordance the words *salvation, save, saved,*
   Savior, deliver, deliverer, delivered, delivers. How, from what, and to what had
   people been saved in the past? How, from what, and to what did people hope
   for salvation?
9. Go back through the book of Nehemiah and pick out key passages or verses to
   memorize. Some passages you might consider are:
     1:4-11, or any part of the prayer that seems significant to you.
     2:17-20
     4:2-5
     4:15
     5:9
     5:14
     6:3
     6:9
     6:13
     6:16
     8:5-6
     8:9-12
     9:5-37, or any part of this confession of faith that touches you, especially
     verses 5-6, 16-17, 27-32.
   You might also consider memorizing Isaiah 44:24,26; 49:14-17; 58:6-7,12; or
   for a balancing word, 9:8-11.

STUDY AIDS

For further information on the material covered in this study, you might consider the following sources. If your local bookstore does not have them, you can have the bookstore order them from the publishers, or you can find them in most seminary libraries. Many college and public libraries will also carry these books.

Commentaries on Nehemiah

Fensham, Charles. *The Book of Ezra, Nehemiah* (New International Commentary on the Old Testament, Eerdmans, 1982).
    More learned use of the Hebrew and other commentators than Kidner's book, although not better researched. A conservative view of author and date. Sound textual comments.

Kidner, Derek. *Ezra and Nehemiah* (Tyndale Old Testament Commentary, Inter-Varsity, 1979).
    Briefer than Fensham by distilling the scholarship down to a vivid view of Nehemiah's character and experience. Available in an inexpensive paperback edition.

Swindoll, Charles. *Hand Me Another Brick* (Bantam, 1981).
    Not strictly a commentary on Nehemiah, but rather a book describing and applying principles of leadership drawn from Nehemiah's example. How to build character in yourself and others. Inexpensive paperback.

Old Testament History and Culture

A Survey of Israel's History by Leon Wood (Zondervan, 1970) is a good basic introduction for laymen from a conservative view point. Not critical or heavily learned for seminarians, but not simplistic.

A *Bible dictionary* or *Bible encyclopedia* alphabetically lists articles about people, places, doctrines, important words, customs, and geography of the Bible.

The New Bible Dictionary, edited by J.D. Douglas, F.F. Bruce, J.I. Packer, N. Hillyer, D. Gutherie, A.R. Millard, and D.J. Wiseman (Tyndale, 1982) is more comprehensive than most dictionaries. Its 1300 pages include quantities of information along with excellent maps, charts, diagrams, and an index for cross-referencing.

Unger's Bible Dictionary by Merrill F. Unger (Moody, 1979) is equally excellent and is available in an inexpensive paperback edition.

The Zondervan Pictorial Encyclopedia edited by Merrill C. Tenney (Zondervan, 1975, 1976) is excellent and exhaustive. It is being revised and updated in the 1980's. However, its five 1000-page volumes are a financial investment, so all but very serious students may prefer to use it at a library.

A good *Bible atlas* can be a great aid to understanding what is going on in a book of the Bible and how geography affected events. Here are a few good choices.

The MacMillan Atlas by Yohanan Aharoni and Michael Avi-Yonah (MacMillan, 1968, 1977) contains 264 maps, 89 photos, and 12 graphics. The many maps of individual events portray battles, movements of people, and changing boundaries in detail.

The New Bible Atlas by J.J. Bimson and J.P. Kane (Tyndale, 1984) has 73 maps, 34 photos, and 34 graphics. Its evangelical perspective, concise and helpful text, and excellent research make it a very good choice, but its greatest strength is its outstanding graphics, such as cross-sections of the Dead Sea.

The Bible Mapbook by Simon Jenkins (Lion, 1984) is much shorter and less expensive than most other atlases, and so it is a good first taste of the usefulness of maps. It contains 91 simple maps, very little text, and 20 graphics. Some of the graphics are computer-generated and intriguing.

The Moody Atlas of Bible Lands by Barry J. Beitzel (Moody, 1984) is scholarly, very evangelical, and full of theological text, indexes, and references. This admirable reference work will be too deep and costly for some, but Beitzel shows vividly how God prepared the land of Israel perfectly for the acts of salvation He was going to accomplish in it.

Yohanan Aharoni has also written *The Land of the Bible: A Historical Geography* (Westminster Press, 1967). After describing the mountains, deserts, winds, rains, and trade routes of ancient Palestine, Aharoni traces the Old Testament history of the promised land with maps and text. For instance, he shows how Abraham lived in Beersheba and how different Judah was from Galilee.

A *handbook* of bible customs can also be useful. Some good ones are *Today's Handbook of Bible Times and Customs* by William L. Coleman (Bethany, 1984) and the less detailed *Daily Life in Bible Times* (Nelson, 1982).

On the Old Testament Law

An exhaustive study from a Christian perspective is R.J. Rushdoony's *Institutes of Biblical Law* (Craig Press, 1973). For comments on particular laws, see commentaries on individual Old Testament books. For instance, J.A. Thompson (*Tyndale Old Testament Commentary*, Eerdmans, 1974) and Peter C. Craigie (*New International Commentary on the Old Testament*, Eerdmans, 1976) both have good commentaries on Deuteronomy.

Old Testament Words

A *concordance* lists words of the Bible alphabetically along with each verse in which the word appears. It lets you do your own word studies. An *exhaustive* concordance lists every instance of every word in a given translation. An *abridged* or *complete* concordance omits either some words, some occurrences of the word, or both.

The two best exhaustive concordances are *Strong's Exhaustive Concordance* and *Young's Analytical Concordance to the Bible*. Both are based on the King James Version of the Bible. *Strong's* has an index by which you can find out which Greek or Hebrew word is used in a given English verse. *Young's* breaks up each English-word listing according to the Greek or Hebrew words it translates. Thus, you can cross-reference the original language's words without knowing that language.

Among other good, less expensive concordances, *Cruden's Complete Concordance* is keyed to the King James and Revised Versions, and *The NIV Complete Concordance* is keyed to the New International Version. These include all references to every word included, but they omit "minor" words. They also lack indexes to the original languages.

The Expository Dictionary of the Old Testament, edited by Merrill F. Unger and William White (Thomas Nelson, 1980) defines major biblical Hebrew words. It is not exhaustive, but it is adequate for the average Bible student who does not know Hebrew.

For Small Group Leaders

How to Lead Small Group Bible Studies (NavPress, 1982).
Just 71 pages. It hits the highlights of how to get members acquainted, ask questions, plan lessons, deal with interpersonal relations, and handle prayer.

The Small Group Leader's Handbook by Steve Barker et. al. (InterVarsity, 1982).
Written by an InterVarsity small group with college students primarily in mind. It includes more than the above book on small group dynamics and how to lead in light of them, and many ideas for worship, building community, and outreach. It has a good chapter on doing inductive Bible study.

Getting Together: A Guide for Good Groups by Em Griffin (InterVarsity, 1982).
Applies to all kinds of groups, not just Bible studies. From his own experience, Griffin draws deep insights into why people join groups; how

people relate to each other; and principles of leadership, decision-making, and discussions. It is fun to read, not highbrow, but its 229 pages will take more time than the above books.

You Can Start a Bible Study Group by Gladys Hunt (Harold Shaw, 1984).
Builds on Hunt's thirty years of experience leading groups. This book is wonderfully focused on God's enabling. It is both clear and applicable for Bible study groups of all kinds.

The Small Group Letter (NavPress).
Unique. Its six pages per issue, ten issues per year are packed with practical ideas for asking questions, planning Bible studies, leading discussion, dealing with group dynamics, encouraging spiritual growth, doing outreach, and so on. It stays up to date because writers always discuss what they are currently doing as small group members and leaders. To subscribe, write to Subscription Services, Post Office Box 1164, Dover, New Jersey 07801.

Bible Study Methods

Braga, James, *How to Study the Bible* (Multnomah, 1982).
Clear chapters on a variety of approaches to Bible study: synthetic, geographical, cultural, historical, doctrinal, practical, and so on. Designed to help the ordinary person without seminary training to use these approaches.

Fee, Gordon, and Douglas Stuart. *How to Read the Bible For All Its Worth* (Zondervan, 1982).
After explaining in general what interpretation (exegesis) and application (hermeneutics) are, Fee and Stuart offer chapters on interpreting and applying the different kinds of writing in the Bible: Epistles, Gospels, Old Testament Law, Old Testament narrative, the Prophets, Psalms, Wisdom, and Revelation. Fee and Stuart also suggest good commentaries on each biblical book. They write as conservative scholars who personally recognize Scripture as God's Word for their daily lives.

Jensen, Irving L. *Independent Bible Study* (Moody, 1963), and *Enjoy Your Bible* (Moody, 1962).
The former is a comprehensive introduction to the inductive Bible study method, especially the use of synthetic charts. The latter is a simpler introduction to the subject.

Wald, Oletta. *The Joy of Discovery in Bible Study* (Augsburg, 1975).
Wald focuses on issues such as how to observe all that is in a text, how to ask questions of a text, how to use grammar and passage structure to see the writer's point, and so on. Very helpful on these subjects.